New Stories from an Old Kid from Wyoming

Robert L. Buenger

iUniverse, Inc.
Bloomington

New Stories from an Old Kid from Wyoming

iUniverse books may be ordered through booksellers or by contacting:

iUniverse
1663 Liberty Drive
Bloomington, IN 47403
www.iuniverse.com
1-800-Authors (1-800-288-4677)

ISBN: 978-1-4620-4088-9 (sc)
ISBN: 978-1-4620-4090-2 (hc)
ISBN: 978-1-4620-4089-6 (ebk)

Printed in the United States of America

iUniverse rev. date: 04/09/2012

Introduction

Indeed we have met again. I sincerely hope that you enjoyed reading my first book, *An Old Kid From Wyoming*, as much as I enjoyed writing it. Today, the world is a whole new kettle of fish, but stories of the glory days never grow old even if their characters do. This book brings back these days from my past through more crazy characters, interesting people, animals, and other situations. Better than fiction, these tales are my life experiences from my eighty years here in Wyoming. If you enjoyed my first book, you will certainly find these new stories an enjoyable and humorous escape from the realities of today.

Acknowledgments

Nick Dudash, an old friend who gave me the artist's conception of the butcher-knife episode

Todd Kahler, who told me to use a professional editor and not a retired schoolteacher who might ruin my voice

Wyoming State Archives, which provided many pictures

CONTENTS

CHAPTER 1

FRONTIER DAYS

No lifetime in Cheyenne would be complete without a full dose of Frontier Days. We all grew up with the promise of this celebration. When we were little, we were all dressed up with hats, boots, loud shirts, wild rags, and whatever our moms could invent.

The best parts at that time were the parades. My mom's aunt, who we called Tanta Elsie, owned a house on the parade route, so we were guaranteed a front-row seat with all the trimmings. At that time, things went on that would put you in jail in today's world. Some of my favorites were the Buffalo Bill floats that had a marksman who would shoot, with an old lever-action rifle, the glass eggs that an assistant would throw into the air. Tiny glass shards would fall out of the air, but people were smart enough to cover their eyes.

A very favorite old lady named Daisey Bristol would always have square dancers performing around her while she played the piano on a float. Daisey had grown up with Cheyenne in the days just after the city had become permanent. Cheyenne was the end of the track for the cross-country railroad that was being built at that time. The part just before Sherman Hill was called Hell on Wheels because it was the highest point on the Union Pacific railroad.

Another favorite was the blacksmith shop's parade entry. An old blacksmith in Cheyenne would shoe a horse throughout the length of the parade.

The Cheyenne Jaycees had a beer-drinking float—for only one year. We tapped a keg at the start of the parade, and we had an authentic looking bar and real-looking cowboys who got really drunk before the parade ended. One of our members was the offspring of a very successful Cheyenne family. Billy had a beautiful pair of pearl-handled revolvers. We got to a corner in the parade, and Billy pulled out both revolvers and started shooting into the air, keeping it up until we were around the corner. We asked him what this was all about, and he said, "My wife was on one corner and my sweetie was on the other. What else could I do?"

There was another old favorite horse lady from Cheyenne. Her name was Mom Chambers. She always rode a beautiful paint horse in every parade. She didn't miss a parade until she was well into her eighties.

The Frontier committee would allow a few select, young cowboys ride back and forth along the edges of the parade. These were always real cowboys, not the Frontier Days type. They would have their ropes in hand, waiting for a choice fair maiden. My sister would always make herself an obvious target.

The early day carriages were maintained by Cheyenne volunteers. The whole town was pretty much committed to the parade presentation. Another float displayed a gold miner at his gold claim. Every once in a while, he would make a big issue of finding a nugget, which was really fool's gold. Then he would throw the nugget to some excited kid along the way.

When I was a little older, it was a big deal to ride a horse with a bunch of other horsemen, just for show. There was not really any big action, but we might be able to have one of the spectators climb aboard with us in any way they could. Another sweltering mission that we would put ourselves through was gaining free admission to the rodeo, if we were tough enough to sit on a saddle horse. These were not choice seats by any stretch of the imagination. We were down the fence from the bucking chutes, so those events were not in our view. The roping chutes were almost directly in front of us, though, so we had a bird's-eye view of the steer roping, calf roping, team roping, and bulldogging. The problem was that we couldn't watch the rough stock. July in Cheyenne was always miserably hot or full of thunderstorms. Either condition was tough to live through, but we thought it was great.

Frontier Nights were always really exciting, with the carnival rides and sideshows. The stage show was a must-see event. They always had strippers, fan dancers, or whatever adolescents were not supposed to see. Admission was limited to adults, but if you were tall enough to see over the ticket window shelf, the people there would accept any lie. Headliners like Mae West, Tempest Storm, and Sally Rand came—really a big deal if you could buy a ticket.

In the arena, some movie star would be on a portable stage. One year, Doc and Festus (from the TV western *Gunsmoke*) were featured and put on a terrific show. They were in their Old West attire. Festus did an Irish jig with the mammoth Mexican rowel spurs on. That, in itself, was spectacular!

Judging from his part on TV playing a tough deputy sheriff, you would never think that his singing voice was worth sour owl shit. Not so! He sang "Danny Boy" with a voice that would tear your heart out.

Before the stage show, while it was still light out, the horse races were a real feature. These were all quarter horses, so none of the races were over the quarter mile. Several different classes of races were held, so there was plenty of betting on horse races.

We always loved the chuck wagon race. Most of the entries were from Canada, but one of the favorites was from Cheyenne. These races started in the middle of the arena. Four chuck wagons were arranged so that each one had an equal distance to run before hitting the racetrack. The position that each racer drew was very important because the inside circle was much tighter than the others. Each wagon was pulled by a "four-up" team, which was four thoroughbred horses. These horses are very high-strung and one is sometimes hard to control—let alone four! Each wagon had four outriders, and two of them would throw the cookstove into the wagon as soon as the starting shot was fired. The advantage went to the first wagon to hit the track and grab the inside lane, closest to the rail. Needless to say, with four 4-horse teams pulling wagons and four outriders for each team, it was a total clusterf—. And these were authentic wagons as far as running gear is concerned. If a wheel came off a wagon in the turn, then drivers, horses, outriders, and equipment would go flying all over the track. This would be a disaster to the racers but out of this world for the spectators.

Frontier Days became a big attraction for the top rodeo contestants, but this wasn't always the case. I knew several old cowboys who would ride the rough stock for five bucks per ride. There were not enough available entrants to make a good show. The early day promoters would hire these riders just to make a good-looking competition. The announcer would tell the crowd, "This is Dale McCloud from Big Sky, Montana," and a few rides later, the same guy would be announced with, "This is Billy Barrow from Virginia Dale, Colorado." They did whatever they had to do to make a show until the real action came around. With bigger prize money, it didn't take long for more rodeos to spring up, along with public interest and more contestants to make rodeo a big business. In the really early days, most of the contestants were from local farms and ranches and had just gotten together to show off their skills. Over the last fifty to a hundred years, rodeo has become a national attraction. More events have been added, and the Professional Rodeo Cowboys Association (PRCA) has done a big number in the sport. Bull riding has become so popular that its participants have organized their own association. Bull riding was never a necessary skill on cattle operation as far as I know, but the event has gone hog wild and has been a huge attraction for rodeos. Many rodeo contestants come from some kind of livestock operation, but today, you can go to school and become a national bull-riding champion without ever seeing a cattle operation.

After the arena night show, we would all head for the dance hall. In those early years, the dance pavilion was mainly just a roof with sidewalls that could be raised in nice weather. Before I was of drinking age, which was mostly regulated by one's ability to walk and talk, one end of the pavilion had open gambling. If a person couldn't walk and talk or look over the bar, he or she was escorted out. At that time, we had orchestras like Lawrence Welk, Eddy Howard, the Dorseys, and other big bands.

The admission to the dance floor was a dime a dance. At the end of each dance tune, four local leaders would walk to the center of the dance floor with ropes tied to each corner. They would go to their respective stations and let you by the rope if you gave them a ticket. We were hometown boys, and these collectors would hand us a few tickets. Most any girl or lady would dance with any guy who had balls enough to ask her or didn't have some big cowboy's objection. As the night wore on, guys' balls would get bigger and bigger. They could even "get lucky, or at least dream about it.

The police would rope off the downtown area, but someone had to really be bad if they took him or her to jail. One night, my brother-in-law made the grade, and I went to bail him out, but the jailhouse was locked. I thought they could have at least put up a "No Vacancies" sign.

The Plains Hotel bar was always packed, and the lobby looked like the rodeo grounds. A stairway to the basement gathered beer cans until it was almost filled by the end of the celebration. We might meet anyone there, including famous people from every walk of life or long lost friends or people we really didn't want to meet. Every now and then, somebody would ride a saddle horse into the lobby because the bar was too crowded. Another one of the places that we had to go to was the Mayflower Bar. Everybody we ever knew might be found there. The place was owned by a Greek family and was always really popular with locals and people who were trying to be locals. We went to school with a son of the owner who was a really good athlete, especially in baseball.

Now, unruly patrons might present a challenge to Phil, and he had no problem with escorting them out the door. I always laughed with Phil about how his nose had been bent in different directions. Of course, anybody who broke Phil's nose was probably in much worse shape himself. My nose was the old classic Nordic nose that was too big of a target. When it got broken, there was so much blood that I couldn't breathe. For this reason, I seldom picked a fight. The story was different with my best friend at the time. We would have spontaneous fights, and he broke my nose more often than I got his.

Frontier Days also always had Bozo the clown. He walked the downtown streets year-round in some sort of clown suit. A good share of the time, he wore a big sandwich board that advertised a local business. But Timber Jack Joe was generally seen only during Frontier Days. He always wore the garb of one of the early day trappers, and his horse was bigger than average.

We didn't see him mounted very often, but when he was, his shepherd dog would ride on the horse's rump above the saddlebags, rifle scabbard, and other survival paraphernalia. I don't go to town during Frontier Days anymore. I'm too damn old, and it ain't what it used to be.

A bunch of friends and relatives always came to visit during Frontier Days. At least one night, we would all go out to the old pavilion and prove once again that we could get drunk while partying. We also spent one night carousing in all the bars downtown. I guess all the magic disappeared when they tore down the old pavilion dance hall.

In the seventies, I was dating Cindy, and we decided to fly from Denver to Cheyenne. The only plane available at Jeffco, which is what we called the local Jefferson County airport, was a little Cessna 152. *Okay*, I thought, *no problem!* We left Denver early to avoid the rough summertime air. As we began our final approach to the airport, Cindy spotted the roping going on in the arena. I took a quick glance right about the time our little plane lost a hundred feet in altitude. We had just flown over one of the small lakes, and the warm air was suddenly gone. I firewalled the throttle, which alarmed the Cinder somewhat, and we landed without further ado.

My sister Sylvia picked us up at the Cheyenne airport terminal and said that she had to take some pictures to her ex-boss. He was at Cloud Nine Lounge and we went there to meet him. A tableful of dignitaries hailed us to join them for a drink. Cinder was quite impressed because she met Governor Herschler and a bunch of National Guard brass. As we wandered around town, she met the mayor, a bunch of old friends, and my sister's best friends, and at the arena, she met Don Kensinger. He always looked very important on his classy-looking saddle horse. We walked a little farther, and I recognized an old friend with his back turned toward us as he worked on an electrical junction box. His name was Myron Wester, but I always called him Hoot. I bellered, "Hey, Hoot! Get over here and meet my new darling!" He recognized my voice, aided by the fact that I called him Hoot. He turned around with a menacing look and dropped his tool belt as if he were about ready to get some revenge. I knew him too well to be concerned, but Cinder didn't know what to think. He got about two feet in front of me with that same menacing look and stuck out his big hand, and a grin that I'd seen so often before spread across his face. A bit of the good times! It was really great to see some of my old friends and introduce my wife-to-be.

My sister's husband, Jimmie, was always active with the Frontier Days Committee and in fact was chairman of the racing committee. There was always a bunch of betting going on, and Jimmie had promoted paramutual betting. It was really successful till the do-gooders voted it down. They said it would promote corruption. I always thought that they didn't want any corruption to interfere with their own.

One year we had a general chairman who claimed he had more authority than the Wyoming governor. Over the years, we have had some great general chairmen, guys who were really interested in the general success of the original spirit. I am really disappointed in the leadership of today. With all the talent that would promote the spirit of Frontier Days, I sincerely detest the decisions to have acid rock groups like Kiss. We may have an earthquake when all the real leaders roll over in their graves.

Those were the days of hard work, an honest handshake, and super patriotism—and the real America!

CHAPTER 2

NAVY EXPERIENCES

My first Navy cruise was aboard the *USS Gunston Hall* LSD-5. I was a brand new Navy Reserve recruit. This was 1948, the war was over, and there were Navy destroyers (some of the smallest seagoing ships in the Navy) moored in Long Beach near San Diego. They were in mothballs, side by side, sixteen wide, and they stretched as far as we could see. There was no doubt in my mind how we had brought the "Rising Sun" to its knees.

We arrived on a Sunday with our seabags in tow. I can't remember how we got to our assigned ship, but we did remember to salute the flag and say, "Permission to come aboard? Sir!"

We weighed anchor in San Diego Harbor the next morning. I got a bunch of experience chipping paint and ignoring any command that started with, "Hey, you. Af ter enduring a night's sleep in a hammock that was at the bottom of four or five tiers, we listened to the boatswains whistle on the intercom: "Toowhheeeyoo! Reveille! Reveille! Clean sweep-down fore and aft!" What a clean sweep-down entailed depended on the individual skipper. This skipper wanted not only a clean sweep-down but also a swab-down. Four to six swab jockeys started at one end of the deck and swung mops while backing up until they met some other crew coming from the other direction.

If our feet weren't on the deck in seconds, some SOB "boats" (Boatswain mate) smacked us on the bottom or our feet. The services were not a kind and gentle place in the late forties! They hadn't heard about rights—civil or otherwise. The old motto "You're in the Army now" was probably nice compared to "You're in the Navy now." The regular Navy had a dry-land boot camp where we got some training in what to expect when we were assigned to a ship, but those of us in the Reserves went directly from dry land (Wyoming) to an oceangoing ship.

This was a little tough. But then, tough was the way we grew up. The experience that we gained in two weeks was enough to make us realize what sacrifices our World War II veterans had made for our country.

I was an SR, or seaman recruit. Once a day, we had a "general quarters" drill. The boatswain would whistle and say, "This is a drill. This is a drill. General quarters. General quarters. All hands to their battle stations." We knew we'd better scamper or somebody would smack us on the butt.

After about the third day, the first-class gunners mate for our battle station bellered, "Who's going to shoot this gun?" He was referring to a 20 mm fully automatic, twin-barrel machine gun. It sounded like a real trip to me. The gunner's mate strapped me into the harness and said, "Shoot it down!" The target was a decoy being towed by a biplane. All I could see was a Japanese "rising sun." Gunny had to grab me and say, "Okay! Okay! Shut it off before you burn the barrel off!" I always loved guns, but I could have become addicted to that one.

We went on several maneuvers from Los Angeles to Long Beach. San Clemente was an island near Catalina that was strictly a Navy training area. We fired our five-inch guns at targets on the island.

A companion ship that carried P boats (landing craft) was in our armada. Its crew launched a bunch of landing craft, and they all headed for our well deck.

The LSD crew would open the floodgate on the aft station, and the ship would sink about twenty feet. The landing craft would navigate in to load up troops, and the LSD crew would close the floodgate to control the wave action. The floodgate was a giant, hydraulic-operated, horizontal, bifold gate that opened the entire transom of the ship to the open ocean. The troops would crawl down a Jacob's ladder (a net-like rope ladder), board the P boats, and ready themselves to hit the beach. This was pretty similar to what the actual troops at Omaha Beach went through, without the murderous gunfire. I have more respect for those soldiers, sailors, and Marines who hit the beach at Normandy than anyone else on earth.

After we had rushed ashore, the command came to "board your boats." We did and were transported back to the ship that we had launched from. Friday night, we got liberty, or official leave from the ship. We had heard about a horseshit and gunsmoke dance hall, so we caught a bus in downtown Long Beach that was supposed to go right by the Sundown Saloon and Dance Hall. Some beneficial soul had told us to tell the driver to let us off on Sundown Avenue. When he did and we departed the bus, it was dark in all directions.

We walked toward the only city lights that might be promising. After an hour or more of walking, we met a big black man and asked, "Where is the Sundown Dance Hall?" He laughed and said, "Man! You a *long* ways from there!" We didn't have any choice but to keep walking. It was almost closing time when we finally got to our destination, but at least we were able to quench a terrible thirst with a couple of beers. No California girls, though.

We got back to our ship before our leave expired, but we were sorely disappointed. Somehow, I had offended some of the deck crew and was assigned to mess cook duties, which was a somewhat demeaning position, but it meant that I could get shore leave liberty every night. I could stand the insult if I got liberty every night. What the hell! It was a weekend, and I called Tanta (Aunt) Elsie. She was a tough old Kraut but asked me to come visit, so I did. I used public transportation to get to her high-style neighborhood in Hollywood. I was really surprised at the mansion that I came to. She gave me a room on the second floor, and most of her other tenants were aspiring actors. As I was taking a bath and relaxing in the community bathroom tub, one of the tenants stepped into the room. With great theatrical fanfare, he pointed at me and asked, "What *is* that?" I couldn't have cared less, and I shrugged my shoulders. Several other "great actors-to-be" appeared on the scene. I was more of a threat to them than they were to me. I was just me, but they wanted to be someone else. I slept well that night and got up before my Shakespearian friends did. Tanta Elsie called me in for potato pancakes; she knew that I was the only person in the vicinity who would enjoy her German dish. We dined and left the other hopefuls to their own.

Tanta Elsie was proud of her sailor nephew, and I was proud to be there. She said, "Let's go to the Hollywood golf course."

"OK," I said. "Why not?"

We got into her beautiful '41 Ford convertible. She said, "I just got it back on Wednesday. Some SOB broadsided me as I backed out of my driveway." She started the engine and, without one glance back, backed onto Hollywood Boulevard. There were tires squealing, horns honking, and plenty of California-style gestures!

Tanta Elsie had only one comment: "Oh, shut up!"

We went about three blocks and came to a stop sign on a steep grade, facing uphill. The engine stalled, and as she was restarting it, we started rolling back down the hill. We gathered more momentum than was comfortable, and I made some mention of the fact. Tanta Elsie said, "If you don't like the way I drive, why don't you drive?" That was the best thing that I had heard all day!

She put on the emergency brake, and we stomped into opposite command posts. I was relieved because her driving put me in more danger than I had ever been in while in the US Navy.

Without further incident, we made it to her Hollywood country club. I wasn't sure if I would be considered "out of uniform" if I took off my dress blue top, but I did and we started our round of golf. We got to the fifth hole, and I hit the ball eighteen times before it quit rolling down to my starting position and landed on the green. Tanta Elsie said, "Don't ever count past five!" The next hole, I eagled.

We had lunch and headed back home, with me driving. As we got to the main thoroughfare, I got in the right turn lane. Tanta Elsie said, "No, no, you want to turn left!" I figured that she had an alternative plan for whatever reason.

We had traveled for ten or fifteen minutes when she said, "You must have passed Wilshire Boulevard."

"Tanta Elsie," I said, "Wilshire Boulevard is back the other way!"

"Oh, you're lost! Pull into that filling station and we'll ask." The attendant said, "You're going the wrong way. It's back west one hundred and forty blocks."

"He doesn't know what he's talking about!" she said as we drove away.

I reversed course about three times and got back on the freeway to the west. Twenty minutes later, Tanta Elsie said, "Just as I told you, there's the Wilshire Boulevard turnoff."

"You sure know where you're going, Tanta Elsie," I said.

"Of course I do!"

I navigated to her mansion and parked her fancy little Ford in her high-dollar garage. It was a fun experience, but I never wanted to try it again. I took public transportation back to LSD-5, which was a relaxing environment compared to my recent domestic experience.

We weighed anchor the next morning and took a south bearing. The skipper of this ship was, indeed, serious about training new recruits. I was on wheel watch, delighted to stand at the "wheel." I was directed to watch the gyrocompass and my heading. After several minutes, the coxswain said, "Go back and look at the wake of your ship." It looked like a snake path. Obviously, I had been oversteering. But no one learns to be a helmsman in one try. I asked for more tries and was awarded several more wheel watches. In a month or so, I might have been a helmsman. but my reserve cruise was too short. Fortunately, it's a big ocean. The feeling it gives is hard to describe. I always loved the vast expanse of the open sea. It might bring you to great fortune, or it might take you to disaster.

The ocean, a big lake, the Laramie Plains Lakes, a beaver pond—they're all close to my heart and would be neat places to cash in my final chips.

I completed my tour of duty with the Navy Reserve. I can honestly say that all the active duty that I served was a great experience, regardless of whatever demeaning things were cast upon me. Because of the lack of experienced electronic technicians who could be mentors, I learned very little that might qualify me for a higher rank. I ended my enlistment as a Seaman ET striker. For five years in the Reserves, this was pretty pathetic. However, I had sailed on both the Pacific and Atlantic Oceans, the Gulf of Mexico and the Great Lakes, and on Navy ships like a landing ship dock, a patrol craft escort, a destroyer, a cruiser, and an aircraft carrier. I had visited Mexico, Canada, Puerto Rico, Guantanamo Bay, and DC. I sometimes wished that I had been called into active service in the Korean "policing action." But then, for what?

CHAPTER 3

THE LAST TRAIL DRIVE

In 1960, the Cheyenne Junior Chamber of Commerce was planning to attend the national convention in St. Louis. I think it might have been some kind of anniversary, but I can't recall at this moment. The Cheyenne and Wyoming Jaycees were very active in that era. In order to belong and be active, people had to be thirty-five years old or younger. If they were older than that, they were "exhausted roosters."

A bunch of us sat in a cocktail lounge, tipping a few drinks and discussing what the Wyoming Jaycees could do to create some interest. A suggestion was made to have the "last cattle drive." People laughed at the idea to start, but then someone said, "Hey, we're the Cowboy State. Why not?" Ambitious young minds started grinding. We could round up a herd of donated critters from some of the big cattle ranchers or whomever we could con into donating. One overambitious Jaycee said, "We could even rustle a few head."

This was a bad thought. We decided that we didn't need any funerals to deal with. People could end up not just exhausted roosters but dead ones.

The dream kept growing. It was presented to the state committee and took off with "great vigor," as JFK would say. Plans kept developing, and it became clear that this was going to happen.

My brother-in-law, Jim McAllister, was president of the Wyoming State Jaycees. He was really enthused and leaned on a bunch of us to make this thing happen. All the Jaycee chapters in the state started accumulating the cattle that we needed. Their efforts turned out to be very successful.

Jim was the proud owner of a Beechcraft Bonanza, which he used to travel to various places so he could help plan ahead. Eventually, we had stockyards, feed, some kind of indoor lodging for our troops, and whatever dining facilities were available. We were set to go!

Our herd was all assembled in Pine Bluffs, Wyoming. Some real cattlemen in Pine Bluffs had already culled the critters that might not make the trip or pose any problem. They were sold at a local livestock auction, and the proceeds helped pay for the trucking. The plan was to drive this herd through the important parts of the cities and truck them in between.

The City of Cheyenne donated a yearling heifer buffalo to take to Busch Gardens as yet another publicity stunt. But how do you load a buffalo? We contacted the appropriate people and found a guy named Elmer. He told us that we should corral the heifer and leave the herd alone for a while. This looked like a hell of a good plan because the big bull was getting pretty upset. He had a bunch of twenty-foot corral poles for toys. He started to hook a horn under a pole and throw it ten or fifteen feet in the air, and Elmer said, "The last time he did that, he also upset my pickup!" When the herd had settled down a little bit, we backed the stock trailer up to the loading chute. The heifer was not too happy about being loaded, but we got her penned off at the front of the semitrailer.

By the time we got to Pine Bluffs, our herders had the big bunch moving toward Bushnell, Nebraska. The only reasons for this drive were to gain publicity and help the herd become a little bit more trail wise.

We loaded in Bushnell and rolled to Lincoln, Nebraska. All went well driving the herd through Lincoln until we got to the loading destination. About five hundred yards before we got to the loading pens, the whole herd spied a lush, green lawn. Seeing eighty head of cattle on its plush lawn was quite disturbing to the management of the large insurance company headquarters. As if this was not bad enough, all the female employees appeared out on the lawn to see the action. Needless to say, a male counterpart showed up immediately. Our only genuine cowboy responded by roping the legs of the managerial person and dragging him a few yards across the lawn. The gals went crazy, screaming and applauding, but the management was very, very disturbed. We lucked out in that no one ended up in jail or named in a lawsuit.

The City of Lincoln arranged for us to house our people in a big dance hall at an amusement park. After feeding our cattle and saddle horses, we proceed to explore the park. Several of us enjoyed ourselves a little later than the rest and got to our bedrolls after everyone else. We had put our gear right next to the piano onstage, and it was completely dark so we weren't bothered with seeking privacy. I was ready to climb into my bedroll when a tremendous gas pain rolled through my guts. I thought that everyone was asleep, so I ripped off a humongous beer fart. Everyone was not asleep, in fact, and the place exploded with laughter and a big round of applause. For the rest of the trip, I had to live down various nicknames.

The next morning, we loaded up and headed to Kansas City. The people at the stockyard there were very helpful, providing the feed and equipment we needed for our cattle and horses. They also provided the National Guard Armory for housing.

There was growing dissent between our president, my friend Jim, and an ambitious young Mexican man whose older brother was the president of the Casper chapter. The young man and Jim met at the exit of the armory, which was about five steps above the surrounding terrain, and exchanged unpleasantries. This young buck was insulted to the point of fisticuffs and took a swing at Jim. Jim flew over the handrail and landed in a trash can. Everyone knew that Jim had a caustic mouth that could provoke such an act. But our young friend apologized, and that matter was over. I knew that this type of thing could happen because I had had to backhand Jim myself over remarks he made about my sister.

Jim and I both had horses, and we had a friend from the western part of the state named Shelby Dill. We were driving Jim's Pontiac station wagon and pulling a double horse trailer. Shelby would drive part time on the road and full time whenever Jim and I were horseback. It was a neat deal. One morning, about dawn, one of our traveling mates thought it would be a good idea to honk his horn in the armory and wake everybody up. He did, and Shelby sat right up in his bedroll and bellered, "Let the son of a bitch go by!" We all cracked up in laughter, but Shelby didn't wake up. He probably thought it was a bad dream.

Our route through Kansas City took us over a viaduct. This caused us all great concern, but it turned out to be quite uneventful. We got into downtown Kansas City and found the streets lined with spectators. A calf that had been born in Lincoln got thoroughly disoriented and left the herd, went toward the crowd, and headed straight for the reflection of himself in the glass facing of a downtown building. A big, black lady was in his path, which scared the poor lady into a panic. She did about a hundred yards worth of running in one place, and the calf ran right past her, hitting the building glass head on at full speed. The poor little guy's legs just sprawled out, and there he lay. A little nuzzling by his mama got him on his feet and back into the drive.

Johnny Foster, our real cowboy, had roped a foxy chick and was promising to snort her flanks. This was what had slowed the drive enough to let our calf episode happen. Johnny was born a hundred years too late. He was an 1860s cowboy. He rode a little black stud horse that he called the Tennessee Stud. I believe this stud horse would have climbed a cliff if Johnny had wanted him to. Johnnie's hat was as black as soot, and the brim had claws embedded in it. We called him Johnny Bearclaw. Anytime the herd was acting right, Johnny set out on the prowl for a pretty young girl. I'm not sure how he kept out of trouble with the law—perhaps because of his boldness. We finished this drive without further incident.

Next, we loaded and headed for Hannibal, Missouri. I can't relay much about the happenings in Hannibal. We had a yearling longhorn steer in the herd that got out of the stockyard, but we caught him before he became completely uncatchable. One of the guys wanted to try a bulldogging maneuver and got the job done. Somebody dared me to ride the steer. I did, but he was pretty spooked and started running straight for a barbwire fence. I wasn't real thrilled about getting into a tangle with a barbwire fence and a longhorn steer. When I stepped off, my boots slipped as if I were on skates because the long, green grass was wet from the morning dew. I was headed for a sure pratfall and put my right hand down to catch myself. *Snap!* I broke my wrist because of a stupid fall like this and was taken to the hospital emergency room. The break was somehow problematic, so the doctor gave me a shot of something to ease the pain and I didn't wake up till the next morning with a cast on my arm. Everybody else was already on the road. The Cheyenne Budweiser distributor was a friend of mine, and he had waited for me to be released from the hospital. He owned a Cessna 210 and flew me down to St. Louis, the site of the convention. The next morning, the mayor wanted to talk to us before we made a drive through his town. Jim and I and a couple of other members of our drive met with him. Jim, who was always thinking ahead, had letters from officials of the other towns that we had been through, but the mayor made it quite clear that we were no longer in the West. St. Louis was the beginning of the eastern United States.

He was concerned that the cattle drive was bigger than what was agreed upon for the Parade of States. Finally, he agreed to allow our drive but warned us to make sure there were no incidents. *Oh, yes, sir, you can depend on us!*

The next morning, we were in the right order to enter the parade. Wyoming, of course, is the last state in the alphabetical listing. Besides this, the city garbage men would follow us to sweep up the inevitable bullshit. We planned an honor guard on horseback to lead our cattle drive and had no problem getting someone to carry the Stars and Stripes. Jim, of course, carried the Jaycee flag, but everyone else was concerned that a fluttering flag could spook his or her horse, so we had no one to carry the Wyoming State flag. I knew that my horse, who I had borrowed from my niece, was not spooked by anything. The only problem was that my arm was in a cast. This didn't seem to be a big problem, though, because my fingers were still suitable for the task with the help of a "flag boot," a simple device that was attached to the right stirrup.

We moved out and our herd followed right behind. The day was miserably hot, and all animals were just dragging along—that is, all but the Brahma bull. This was his type of weather. This Brahma had been a calf for the Pine Bluffs calf-roping team, and somehow, one of his front legs had gotten broken. He was nursed back to health and became as tame and gentle as a Brahma could be. During the trip, we had all petted or scratched this giant animal.

The parade was moving along well until one of the renegade pseudo-cowboys from the coal mining country decided he wanted to put on a show by bulldogging our longhorn yearling. His partner twirled his rope to catch the yearling so that Mr. Macho could show off. The big problem was that he twirled his rope right over the head of our Brahma, who was enjoying the sweltering weather and decided to make a run for it.

Everybody started to beller for Johnny Bearclaw, who was in the process of mugging a foxy young chick. He heard the screams and came running, full tilt, on the Tennessee Stud. He chased the Brahma about a block and a half and dabbed his rope on the critter. The Brahma had had his fun and was led back to the herd with no further problem. Without our true cowboy, I'm sure that the only solution would have been a dead Brahma.

The parade ended uneventfully. All the livestock, except the Brahma, were near exhaustion. After we got all the critters loaded, we took advantage of the fire hydrants that the St. Louis Fire Department had opened for us. Most of us were able to get hoses to wash down our horses, so we pull off the saddles and let the cool water run all over them.

Our cattle drive was over, and everybody let out a big sigh of relief. We got a nice check from the St. Louis Stockyard Commission that covered most of the expenses.

A bunch of individual stories should have been written about that drive, but to my knowledge this is the only one.

Chapter 4

THROUGH THE BEST OF IT

There are places like Lake Creek, Blackwater Creek, Cape Hatteras, Devil's Gate, Canada, Panama, the Douglas, and so on. In the US Navy, there were cruisers like *USS Albany* (CA-123) and aircraft carriers like the *USS Leyte* (CV-32). In transportation, there are feet, horses, cars, trucks, boats, aircraft, and the seat of your pants. There are fishing and hunting trips, parties, business deals, partnerships, accidents, failures, and successes—plenty of experiences and adventures. All of my adult life I have shared with a special friend.

Some of these epics are related herein.

I met John at the Cheyenne unit of the US Naval Reserve. We were of similar demeanor, interests, and lifestyle. John was an electrician apprentice, and I was an apprentice in the carpentry trade. At that time a young man could not learn a trade without being associated with the appropriate union. Both of us were single at the time but were pretty well committed to a couple of foxy young gals and headed for wedlock.

We went on a Navy cruise to the Great Lakes and were assigned to a USS PCE, or Patrol Craft Escort. We had a few hours to kill before being transported to Naval Station Great Lakes. As we were walking toward the bright lights, a neat-looking convertible stopped and blocked our forward progress. Lo and behold, it held two fair maidens. I said something ridiculous, and the fair maidens sped off. Young sailors are supposed to be very cool in situations like this. I was not. We ventured on and started to pass a local pub, in which there was obviously a rollicking party. We decided to go in and ordered a couple of drinks, and the bartender filled our order, waving off any payment. We went along with this unusual situation until a huge, uniformed Marine appeared before us. He asked for our invitations to the wedding reception that was going on. We offered to leave *post haste*! His face indicated that an immediate retreat was being demanded, and we complied in a very efficient manner. Having had enough for one night in Chicago, we caught our transportation to our seagoing home for the next two weeks.

This fleet was made up of four PCEs, and the flagship was a destroyer escort. Most of the crew was regular Navy, and the balance was made up of Navy Reserve sailors. The regular Navy crew members were mostly old salts. I think that all of them had been really good sailors at one time or another but had been reassigned to this duty to serve out their enlistments. The few guys who I got to know had held much higher ranks but had been busted for some unexplained reason. The captain's name was Mr. Fish, and the executive officers name was Mr. Bone. I never knew if these names were authentic or acquired.

The cruise was pretty uneventful, but we did get liberty in Canada and got to see our salty old captain prevent a collision in a seagoing mail-passing drill. We also witnessed a third-class boatswain's mate tell the fleet admiral to shut his mouth and get back to his bunk where he belonged when he interfered with the docking maneuver that the "boats" were in full command of. We went on two other reserve cruises and were fortunate enough to draw a carrier and a cruiser for further naval training.

A fishing trip that was of some interest was one that we went on in the early spring to the Devil's Gate Crick. The trip into this colorful spot wasn't too bad except for the fact that we came very close to tumbling into a beaver dam.

I remember standing on the passenger-side running board, trying to keep a positive center of gravity. On the way out, we met two totally inexperienced adventurers who were completely without appropriate tools, vehicle, clothing, and food. Apparently, the thought that the bottom of the mountain was somewhat more difficult to get out of than it was to slide into had never occurred to them. That area was completely void of any general stores, motels, gas stations, or other conveniences that may be needed for any extended stay. The two said they planned to "live off the land." They said that they had started down the road and couldn't go back up. Not good survival planning! We were in John's '41 Ford pickup with tire chains and were having a little trouble going up the road. After all, it was only a Forest Service fire road.

My friend's pickup was always meticulously equipped for any job. Between the two of us, we were able to get those two dudes out of the valley in the snowstorm. We knew—even if they didn't—that we had saved them from a lot of misery, a giant rescue mission, and maybe the loss of their lives. The off-road valleys can be very unforgiving at any time of the year in Wyoming.

After this little distraction, we thought that we were very lucky to find an abandoned log cabin. We pulled out our fart sacks and spent a very comfortable night. At sunrise, it was a very different story. The sun was shining as strong and warm as anyone could imagine. The only problem was that there was no roofing, and the roof sheathing boards were spaced four or five inches apart. With the sun melting the piled-up snow, we found ourselves in a downpour. No problem! We just threw our wet sleeping bags in the back of the pickup and proceed to cook breakfast. Problem! We had lost the coffee pot in all the activities the night before. Our very simple solution was to eat a full can of pork and beans so that the can could serve as a coffee pot. Our first course of breakfast was just a tad pasty, but the coffee was sure good. And we had our choice of some of the best trout fishing streams in Wyoming. Going from snowstorm to sunny day is no strange phenomenon in Wyoming.

In our youth, we did goofy things just to prove that we were somewhat different than our peers. When we were drinking beer, we had to practice the custom of "having an egg in your beer." (meaning living big by by drinking a raw egg in your glass of beer.

At the Frontier Days night shows, we were well supplied with either a keg of beer or a mixture of gin and several other ingredients, and we called it redeye.

In the early years, we applied our skills to build one another's family houses. I was always indebted to John because he has stayed in his home to the present day, but I have built seven houses for two wives and John has wired most of them.

Our kids were always in the scene; however, John and Bonita had five and my first wife and I produced only two. It was a pleasure to see these young guys grow up and brag about their accomplishments. Raising kids during the sixties was a real challenge, but ours turned out to be solid citizens instead of the misguided young people of that era. Ours all weathered the storm and turned out to be great. Some of them have produced grandkids and great-grandkids. My own immediate family was sadly and heartbreakingly on the decline because of premature deaths. John and Bonita, with all of their offspring and relatives, definitely made my life more bearable. Their entire family accepted me as part of their own.

By 1968, I had moved to Denver because I had sold our home and the prospects for success in my building business were very slim. We had succeeded in our ventures for several years, and my new wife, Cinder, and I moved to Gillette. After several years of building rental buildings, John invested with me and we developed two more properties. Everything looked great until the eighties almost wiped us out. I went to Las Vegas to help make payments on our properties. John took over the management of our properties and invested a very considerable amount of money and time to prevent foreclosure. In due time, we both got our additional investments back and were able to make a success of this whole deal.

I could go on enough to fill another book with the deeds and misdeeds of our friendship. I can honestly say, without question or afterthought, that no man has ever had a better friend.

CHAPTER 5

CHERYL AND RICK

I would wish that all the people in the world could be as happy as I have been and live a life that is as fulfilled as mine has been. I have beaten the odds! That's not to say that there were not devastating happenings along the way. My young adult life was filled with the loss of a grandfather, a grandmother, and a favorite uncle, all within one year. The premature death of my dad was almost more than I could handle. We all had such a great future ahead if only Dad had been with us for a normal lifetime. My mom, sister, and niece Patsy were all that was left. Fortunately, I had started a new family, and my dad got to hold my daughter Cheryl before he passed away. He would have been the happiest man in the world if he had lived long enough to enjoy his grandkids Patsy, Cheryl, and Rick. A few years later, Patsy died giving birth to a son. Unfortunately, this event all but destroyed my sister, Patsy's mom. I don't think that she lived another really happy day until the day of her own death in 1996.

Enough of this sadness!

Cheryl just grew up way too quickly. I never had any trouble with my teenage daughter, who was making her own history with high school grades and the debate program. This was during the time that I was making a big change in my ability to support my family.

My mother gave Cheryl a nickname—Toots—and only a grandmother could explain why.

When we sold the house that I had built for my young family, we moved into an apartment near the Trinity Lutheran Church. Both Cheryl and Rick were baptized there; it had been my family's church for years. Our favorite minister was Reverend Nierman. Cheryl took a special liking to him when she was only five or six years old. We lived about two blocks from the church, and Cheryl would get up on Sunday mornings and walk to Sunday school, which let out at the same time as the service. Cheryl would run to the front door and hold Reverend Nierman's left hand while he greeted the departing members. Years later he, of course, officiated Cheryl's wedding. He told me at the reception that a little tear had run down his cheek during the ceremony. As far as I am concerned, he was the last true man of God that I ever knew. I'm sure that Toots feels the same way.

Toots had her dreams of going off to a school other than the University of Wyoming, and if we had known the success that my new venture would bring, we probably would have been able to give her that opportunity. As it happened, she went to the University of Wyoming and ended up with degree as a medical technician and a husband whom she supported while he earned his master's degree.

When her new husband graduated, they moved to Denver, and Toots went to work in her medical training field, becoming a leader in new treatments of blood engineering. The next thing I knew, she told me that she was going to make me a grandfather. This took me by complete surprise; it took me a short time to get used to the idea.

She, in turn, faced a few disasters that she handled with the super strong character that she had always displayed. She had always been a reading fanatic, and she became a published author. She enjoyed using this talent and published quite a few books, but she got tired of the pressure from the publishers.

My granddaughter was born and became the start of a brand new life.

But the memories of the games that Toots and I played when she was little came back quite vividly. One involved a soap opera on which we heard about the troubles of a soapy couple. During their agony, they would sigh at each other, "Oh *John*," and then, "Oh *Marsha*." We would mimic their pathetic groans at least once a day and then laugh heartily. She also had an imaginary friend named Beca who I would send off to California or kick out of the house. She could always find Beca at my sister's house. If I could get her away from a book, we played silly games like these.

Now her granddaughter—my great-granddaughter—has been born and become the newest delight. Cheryl has found a new job that matches her talents and is near her granddaughter in Michigan. My only problem with this is that they are farther away from me, but this is all right because they are really content.

My son Rick was another story. We built all kinds of things together, from toy boats to houses and shop buildings. He had served his apprenticeship as a carpenter by the time he was ten.

A favorite memory of Rick's younger days was a comment he made when he was only about three. My wife and I were lying in bed one Sunday morning when the kids came in and jumped in bed with us. I noticed that Rick was studying my significant countenance! Pretty quickly, he said, "Dad, when I grow up, I want to have a nose just like yours!" He didn't quite make it, but he got close. I was certainly glad that Toots wasn't burdened with it.

The only sport he played, besides hunting, fishing, and skiing, was Little League baseball. He is a southpaw and could burn a catcher's hand with his pitches in his first year. When we first realized what kind of arm he had, he could be really on or really off. I worked with him every day, and he developed a mean slider. The ball would slide in toward a right-handed batter or away from another lefty. His crowning glory occurred when he was a relief pitcher coming in for a starting pitcher who had loaded the bases. He pitched a no-hitter to win the series in his league. His baseball career came to a halt the next year because, like his dad, he couldn't get along with the coach.

He was certainly a crack shot with a rifle, especially considering how much we got to shoot together, but he focused on gun safety from the first time that he touched one. Water skiing was one sport that he really loved. Because of some stupid actions on my part, we couldn't afford a boat. But relatives of my first wife Glenna in Laramie were happy to furnish a boat for us. We used to go to Guernsey Lake with them every summer, but when Bobby Yeoman's boat was unavailable, Rick was known as the hitchhiker. He'd stand on the shoreline in knee-deep water with his slalom ski and wait for some boaters to come by and throw him a rope.

We got along as a father and son should until I started working in Denver. Sadly, this was probably the time that he needed me most. Those were the days of the hippie; teachers were teaching that anyone over thirty was extremely prejudiced and couldn't be trusted. The Kennedy assassination had just occurred, a move from Cheyenne was happening, his sister was away at college, and he had to enter a new school where dope was running rampant,

The Jefferson County schools could not accept the fact that a Cheyenne student was advanced at schooling, especially in math. I talked to Dr. White, the principal of Rick's new school, and he told me that Rick could not be in a calculus class. I challenged his statement and asked him to show me Rick's record. Sure enough, I was right. He told me that they would really challenge him the next year. Bullshit!

The whole episode that followed was enough to drive me crazy. This was my son! Rick was never challenged after that and gave up on high school. After a few bizarre episodes, he came to work for me and took over the prefab crew. He'd complete whatever was needed for a few days in advance and then choose not to work for a day or so. Bobby Calhoun was running a particular project and was always concerned about work ethics. He expected his crew to show up every day on time. He kept telling me that Rick was worth much better wages but that he couldn't justify giving him a raise. Rick kept telling me that he knew that he was worth better wages and that Bobby wouldn't give him a raise. What we had there was a pure-dee Mexican standoff! I was right in the middle, and I was the big boss! I wouldn't undermine Bobby's authority, and I couldn't make my son understand that we all knew that he was doing his job but that work ethics were just as important.

Rick worked with me for a while, and then the developer that we were working for offered him a job as a project manager. This only lasted as long as it took Rick to tell the company manager how poorly the whole company was being run. Another developer recognized Rick's ability, took him on, and treated him very well, including giving him a share in his development company.

During all this, Rick got married and fathered another super granddaughter for me. This marriage didn't work out, though, and Rick decided to go get a college degree. He did, graduating something *cum laude*.

Again, he was sought after to supervise a commercial building and restaurant. He finished the job in record time but was, again, too much for his boss. Rick met a classy lady at some ballroom dance affair, and they quickly moved through the best friend, soul mate, and matrimonial modes. It took a while, but they have melded into a near perfect couple. They compiled their finances and built a mansion with a fantastic dance floor. Stephany had gained experience in jobs with very high security clearances, and right now she is in line for a high-ranking defense contractor position. In addition, she is really a neat daughter-in-law.

I am really proud of my son and daughter, but wait! There's more.

Sarah, my first granddaughter, and I bonded very early in her life. She was part of Rick's wedding ceremony, but she freaked out. She needed somebody who was not part of the ceremony. She went running down the aisle, passed two grandmothers' outstretched arms, and jumped into mine. There was no doubt about where we stood in each other's lives from then on. After the Cinder and I were married and moved to Gillette, she came to visit for a while almost every summer. When we had a small farm-ranch in Powell, Wyoming, she was still pretty small and I started to call her Peewee. This endearing name has stayed with her through her adult years. Now, she and her husband both tower over Grandpa. Those years in Powell were some of the best in my life. Sarah and I were almost inseparable, and the memories are indelible.

Sarah has had a few disastrous events in her young life, but she heeded my words when I told her that everyone has some disastrous events in their lives but what's important is how we handle them. She has always performed with great courage and strength of character. We are bonded forever. Sarah chose Northwestern University and graduated with honors. She was then accepted at Harvard Law School. Cinder and I just had to attend her graduation, and it was significant because it was held in the first rainstorm to occur during the ceremony in something like a hundred years. We had to laugh that people in one of the best gene pools in the world didn't have enough sense to come in out of the rain. Their mortar boards all drooped sadly. Sarah later married a young man named JJ who had many different degrees. After Sarah had served as a federal judge assistant, the two of them moved to Michigan, where JJ became a law professor at the University of Michigan and Sarah began working as a trial lawyer in a prestigious law firm in Detroit.

Another great event in my life was the birth of Emily, my son's daughter. I wasn't able to have Emily as close as Sarah, but this didn't diminish our relationship. I was in Las Vegas most of the time that Emily was little, but I took some time to see her and my sister. One weekend started with a performance of the Lipizzaner Stallions in Colorado. After the show, Emily and I went up to my sister Sodie's house in Cheyenne for a few days. I think that this was the first time that Em had been away from home. Everything was going great until Sodie's old dog wandered off. Big panic! This old dog might wander onto the busy street in front of the house. The sudden excitement sent Em screaming into the house. I went in after her, and she was terrified, saying, "I'm scared of outside!" I picked her up and calmed her down a little. I said, "Emily, you're with your grandpa, and nothing can happen to you. We've got a job to do. You don't need to be afraid of anything!" Since that little incident, I can't remember her being afraid of anything. I think at that moment we bonded, and we've had a bunch of adventures ever since.

I took Emily to a Barnes and Noble bookstore a few years later to buy her a birthday present. She has always been a bookworm, just like her aunt Cheryl, so a trip to the bookstore was always an all-day event. I tried to keep track of her, and each time I would find her in a different aisle, sitting down and reading whatever book that interested her at that particular time. After an hour or four, I found her in the comic aisle. She had a book or two picked out from other aisles but wanted a couple from the Garfield selection. I asked a foolish question: "Why don't you read some classics of some kind?" She said, "Like what?" I got carried away and said, "Oh, something like *The Odyssey* and *The Iliad*." She replied, "I've read them." I wanted to quiz her more but knew she would outsmart me.

Em came down to Las Vegas by herself one time, and we went to the Water World park. She said that she wanted to go down the Superslide. It was a double enclosed-tube waterslide that was about three or four stories high, and the tubes twisted around each other. She jumped in one side, and I had to jump in the other. It was a hell of a trip for an aging grandpa and a little kid! But that wasn't enough; we had to plunge into the Black Hole, a ride designed to simulate a mammoth whirlpool. The signs along the walkway warned us of a claustrophobic effect. We jumped into an inner tube-type sled, and away we went. The thing damn sure made the ride realistic.

Since that time, she became the valedictorian of her high school and fulfilled a scholarship for her bachelor's degree, earning a full-ride scholarship at Duke University. In her high school speech, she said that she was going to make the world a better place. She will!

And now, there is another little person to be dealt with—Annelise, Sarah's new baby. History begins again. With all the pundits in her immediate gene pool, maybe she will heal some of the scars that humanity has bestowed upon itself. Right now, she is perfect and we can only hope. In the meantime, we will enjoy what she brings day to day.

Since I wrote this chapter, we found out that our family has another baby on the way. This will be the first boy born to our family in over fifty-five years!

CHAPTER 6

DOONEY

A friend of mine from the word go, Dooney's real name was Donald Lamb, but he was Dooney to all his friends. I don't know of anybody who knew Dooney that like didn't him. This feature was especially nice when my old buddy Mid and I were sophomores in high school. Dooney knew a bunch of senior girls and fixed us up with any one of them we asked him to. All three of us hung around with each other that whole year, along with all the girls that Dooney knew.

The next year, Dooney joined the Army and we didn't see much of him for the next four years. When he returned, Dad invited him to stay at our house—"The Buenger Hotel."

At that time, my dad had retired from Wallick and Buenger, the company Dad had started with Jack Wallick. They had made a giant success of it, but Dad got tired of the whole situation.

Dad was always starting new businesses, and at that time he had developed a roofing-materials manufacturing business along with an artificial-stone veneer business. Dad knew Dooney and his ability—and his personal ethics—so he hired him immediately.

Dooney and I worked together on all kinds of projects until Dad died in 1953. This pretty well ended the business, and Dooney went to work for a furniture company. It was a really big disaster for all of us. A few years later, Dooney said, "Can you imagine how much our lives would have changed if your dad hadn't died so young?"

We had a very close relationship for the next few years. Dooney married my friend's sister, Betty, and our kids were all born within the following several years. We watched them grow up during the sixties, not a good time to raise kids.

Dooney loved fishing and pheasant hunting. We had done a few jobs with the farmers in pheasant country, and all of them and a bunch more welcomed Dooney to their farms. That was his way of life—meet somebody and enjoy the meeting for years.

Dooney and my brother-in-law and I were doing a four-story job in Casper on one of the busiest intersections in town. As we built our scaffold higher, the more we could see the hiked-up skirts of the passing drivers and passengers. This became a constant distraction. One warm summer day, we were hard at work when Rex, my brother-in-law, walked around our work shelter and stumbled over thirty-some-odd cans of our stone sand. It was one hell of a crash.

Dooney was always nervous with Rex around, resulting in high tension. About three seconds after Rex's crash, I got distracted by some skirts and bumped a thirty-two-inch stone form off of my three-story scaffold. It crashed to the sidewalk. Dooney had had enough. He bellered, "I quit! You sons of bitches are trying to kill me!" Years later, this whole scene came back to me when Dooney's son Alan was helping me with the siding on the house in Cheyenne that I was building for Cinder and me when we were finally moving back from Las Vegas. I was on a scaffold on the side of our house and knocked a plank off the top section. It went crashing down to the ground, and I was pleased to see that Alan was well clear of it. I had attempted to warn Alan of my poor safety habits, but my warnings were not needed. Alan grinned and held up his hand to stop me, saying, "I know all about you!" Alan was the same type of person as his dad.

Dooney, Mid, and I were once at Hawk Springs Reservoir on a fishing trip. We had our rubber raft blown up and pushed off from shore. Dooney had warned us about the wind, but we carelessly ignored him. It was worse that even Dooney expected. The wind caught us, and no amount of paddling would take us back to shore. We ended up on the other side of the lake and had to walk back to our pickup. Dooney didn't say a thing, but we had to withstand the wrath in his eyes and face. One day, at the store where Dooney worked, General Carson came in to make a purchase. We had all been on pheasant hunting trips together. The store owner was impressed that the general was in his store and had several salespeople in attendance. General Carson saw Dooney and made a special effort to say, "Hi, Dooney." Dooney said, "Hi, Dick," just as casually as that. He was just that kind of guy.

Dooney and his wife Betty spent a lot of time fishing and always had fish in their freezer. When Cinder and I first got back, he brought over a nice little batch of our favorite fish and a bunch of flower seeds for our yard. These have become "Dooney flowers," and they will always be in our yard

I'm sure that I will never know anybody as likeable as Dooney and his kinfolk.

CHAPTER 7

PAPPY

My first father-in-law was the source of a very controversial issue. The first words that Pappy ever said to me were on an evening that I had come by to pick up his daughter and my future wife, Glenna. "You're pretty regular around here, kid!" he said. Rex, Glenna's younger brother, eased the situation by saying, "Don't pay any attention to him," but it was pretty obvious that this guy said whatever was on his mind.

Over the many years that I knew Clyde Beougher, he never ceased to amaze me. As far as his work ethic was concerned, he towered over all. For being one of the "old school" carpenters, he wouldn't hesitate a second to try a new idea that might speed up a particular process. He could build something, screw it up by trying to make it better, tear it down, and build it back in half the time that the average carpenter took to build it in the first place. If anyone went to the outhouse on the job, he had better be quick or he could be accused of "shit arrest." Clyde's "get it done" (even if you had to do it again) attitude gave us the confidence to "just do it." But we knew we had to get it done.

I think that Clyde's dad was a carpenter, and I know that his father-in-law (the original Pappy) was. The building trades were pretty ingrained in this family. I guess the Pappy title was just handed down from generation to generation. I do know that we didn't start calling Clyde "Pappy" until some years after the other one died, probably around the time Clyde was closing in on being a great-grandfather.

A bunch of bricklayers were in the family, as were railroad boilermakers and machinists. We cursed, overcursed, precursed, and probably triple-cursed one another. If someone couldn't handle it, he was doomed. Pappy would be mad and chew someone out royally one minute, and the next he'd say something like, "Let's knock off early and go fishing."

After I had become the boss (only because I signed the paycheck), I hired an ornery old carpenter under whom I had served some of my apprenticeship, Bob Graber. He was almost as grouchy as Pappy. We were building the Warren Livestock office building in Cheyenne when the words started flying at an atrocious rate. An electrician friend came up to me and said, "You've got a couple carpenters that are about to get in a fight!" I told him, "I hope the hell they do. Maybe one of them will shut up." They didn't.

Pappy was a great one to lecture on the virtues of a "relaxed grip" on a hammer, a golf club, a fishing pole, or whatever. One downside is that I have witnessed all of these tools flying through the air—maybe he was just a tad too relaxed. I guess the only sport that we didn't share was golf, but I heard about a particular event. Pappy was set to drive across a small lake at the Cheyenne Airport golf course. He teed up and took a mighty swing, sending the golf club almost half as far as the ball and into the lake. Rex was recruited to dive for the club and came up with the club plus a season's worth of balls.

Another time, we were fishing in a Snowy Range lake and Pappy had a new spinning reel. The fishing was good, and Pappy was getting more enthusiastic with every cast. The inevitable "gawd da-yamm" was heard when Pappy's relaxed grip had just allowed his new pole and reel to go overboard. With youthful exuberance, I told Pappy, "No problem. I'll dive down and get it." I hadn't considered the fact that my ancestry didn't include a polar bear. I had stripped down to my birthday suit, and when I slid over the side of the boat, my involuntary gasping convinced me that I had made an overconfident statement. Pappy and my friend Johnny Kahler pulled me back into the boat, and we drove back to Laramie to buy Pappy a new fishing outfit.

I've seen him at the tiller of one of our fishing boats, fishing, steering, baiting hooks, and building a new long chain of spinners. He'd have it complete with the bait on and then bring his line in to change outfits. He'd snap off the old gear and throw the new one over the side without tying it onto his line. "Well, gawd da-yamm!" he'd say. We could see it coming every time but didn't warn him.

We were sheathing the roof on a house one time, and Pappy had just gotten a new pair of bifocals. He walked down to the edge of the roof to get another board. Still getting used to his new vision, he still saw roof to walk on and took a header straight to the turf below. I don't know why he didn't break his ornery old neck, but when we started down the ladder to help, he bellered, "Get your blankety-blank asses back up there and finish that roof!" Then he drove himself to the hospital and was in traction for a week or two.

Some of the earliest fishing trips with Pappy involved an ultralight boat that he and an aircraft mechanic had made. The frame was aircraft aluminum tubing, and it was covered with canvas and paint, just like the early Pipers and Cessnas. We transported it to the lake on a car-top carrier. Two guys could easily carry it to the water, but it handled four fishermen with ease.

We took an annual trip to Sand Lake in the Snowy Range. By breakfast time, we would have a nice mess of eastern brook trout. All the dudes in camp would see our fish and immediately go rent a boat from Gene Alloway's little fleet. They didn't realize that they were too late to start and would quit before the fishing got good again. They didn't have the bag of tricks that Pappy had taught us.

Pappy and I and another carpenter were shingling a roof one windy day. My flatulence was widely known, but I was often blamed for something that I did not do. A customary method of shingling is for each shingler to take five or six courses across at a time. I had the lead and was about ten feet downwind of Pappy. Don, our carpenter, was about ten feet upwind of Pappy. All of a sudden, Pappy went into a tantrum. With great indignation, he bellered, "Gawd da-yamm, Pink! You can fart against a forty mile an hour wind!" Don doubled over with laughter, knowing that I had taken another bad rap.

Profanity was no problem for Pappy. He had spent too much time near Texas, where the first thing a child learns in grade school is to make a declarative sentence without the word *shit*. Most people didn't pay much attention because his dialogue just flowed together so emphatically and naturally. But there was always the inevitable uppity-puppity who would take great offense. When that happened, it was the uppity-puppity who had to leave, not Pappy.

Pappy bought a new Mercury four-door sedan in the early fifties. It was a beautiful silver color and was his pride and joy. He always took good care of possessions unless there was something more important that needed his attention. At one point, we were antelope hunting in the Red Desert and had three or four vehicles. We had spotted a herd and planned our strategy. I was to take a road around the back side of a long ridge and maybe bugger them over the other ridge toward Pappy and crew. When we got far enough, I topped the ridge and could scarcely believe my eyes. I saw what looked like a silver torpedo blowing shoulder-high brush in every direction. The herd had crossed the draw and gotten out of sight, but Pappy wasn't about to let that happen. I don't remember whether anybody got a shot, but I was sure the new Mercury was going to be a wreck. But cars were built with a lot of iron in those days, and miraculously the new Mercury suffered only a few scratches.

In all the years that we worked together, fished and hunted together, got cursed by and cursed at each other, I discovered a few things: Pappy was an honest, evil, inconsiderate, kind, crooked, and trustworthy-to-the-death critical mentor. I could love him one minute and hate him the next. I'm not too sure why we didn't kill one another—probably because of what I knew about Pappy and what he didn't know about me. He was a walking contradiction, and he was my friend.

CHAPTER 8

BILL—JUST PLAIN BILL

For one reason or another, I never knew a "just plain" Bill. The first Bill that I ever knew was Bill Brolliar. We met in first grade, at Park Addition Elementary School, continued our friendship through Clark Elementary, and somehow have communicated for better than a half century. We used to spend a weekend night together and imagine all kinds of strange tales. Billy moved around Cheyenne a few times and then moved to Fort Collins, Colorado, but we stayed in touch. I remember that several times during this relationship, I would realize that I had not had contact with him for up to fifteen years. Then I would get a phone call, and the caller would say, "Pink, this is Bill!" Somehow I knew, every time, that it was Billy Brolliar.

The last time I saw Billy was around 1980. He and his older brother were near Cheyenne and Cinder got to meet one of my earliest friends at my sister Sodie's house. Bill was an entrepreneur and, as far as I know, was always very successful. He had an older brother who was greatly talented in the art field. In the late thirties, Boyd sculpted a snowman bust of Thomas Jefferson. This was not an average snow sculpture. It was more than eight feet tall and was more accurately detailed than anything I ever remember seeing. He was only in his teens.

Billy Christensen was another first-grade acquaintance. His family was a big part of the local dairy industry. His dad ran the dairy ranch, one uncle processed and delivered the milk products, and another uncle was just a rough, tough, fun-loving old cowboy.

It was a great trip for me to ride the school bus with Bill and spend the night at his dad's dairy farm. Every time I went out there, we caught their Shetland pony. We always faced the decision of who would "top him off" (ride him first). It could be Bill, Buster, Barbara, or Bingo (yours truly). I always thought that I got the honor a disproportionate number of times, but they were always laughing with me, not at me. Bill's younger brother Buster became a carpenter and worked for me on several occasions. Bill's sister—not sure if she was younger or older—caught my eye and heart on several occasions. Also, I seldom found Bill to be looking for a fight; the fights always seemed to find him. The last time I saw Bill alive, he said to me, "If I walk into a building with ten thousand people, one of them will be looking for a fight and he'll find me." His problem was that his fists were the only diplomacy that he had.

Now Bill Van Zee, another fighter with a couple of foxy sisters, was somewhat different. With just a little provocation, he would be in a fight. I was somehow lucky enough to avoid any confrontation with these two guys. It wasn't that I was a bad fighter; it was just that my big sauerkraut snazoon gave any opponent an unfair advantage.

Bill Gavin was married to a friend of my first wife. He was a railroad conductor and probably one of the most pleasant people I've ever known. Somehow, a Frontier Days event could have become quite violent. Bill and I had been enjoying the late July evening and were following the lead of our stylish mates, heading toward the popular Elk's Club bar and dance hall. During Frontier Days, the traffic is always stop and go on both the streets and sidewalks.

In the street, across two lanes of traffic, came wolf whistles and suggestive sexual remarks aimed at our wives. It was easy to tell that the remarks came from a carload of would-be cowboys. Bill didn't say a word or give me any idea of his intentions. He merely walked across the two lanes of traffic, opened the door, grabbed the pseudo-macho driver by his collar, jerked him out of his seat, lifted him off the ground, and said, "Why don't you guys apologize to those ladies across the street." I was right behind Bill, but I'm sure that my presence had little to do with the various apologetic comments that came blurting from that car. The cool and calm demeanor wouldn't scare too many, but the sight of a leader suspended by his necktie and doing a little toe dance in the middle of Central Avenue made a pretty impressive scene. Just plain Bill? Hardly.

In the early seventies, I hired a tall, clean-looking hippie named Billie Brashears. At that time, employers didn't have any idea who they really may have hired. He said that he was from Cheyenne, and I wasn't sure that this meant anything. He was definitely different from the average goon who walked up on the job. My superintendent of derelicts, Darryl, had informed me that he needed more help, so I told Billie to report to Darryl's job the next morning. Billie fit in with this crew, and it took Darryl no time to put this new hand in charge of the roof framing crew. I think that Billie was sure that he could fly.

One morning, I got a call that Billie had reached for the forklift load of sheathing and missed. He took a header straight into the spring mud and was out like a light. Darryl said he had thought about attempting resuscitation but called 9-1-1 instead. The EMTs were taking care of Billie almost as soon as he hit the ground.

We were greatly concerned, but had to wait for the medical report. About three thirty that afternoon, I got a call from the hospital. "Please come and pick up this wild hippie"

Billie was no worse for the crash. When I signed him out, I questioned my own judgment. Billie had stirred up enough trouble and excitement that the hospital staff wanted to get rid of him as soon as possible. I wondered if we would be wise to do the same. I don't remember how long he worked for us, but it was a thrill a minute. And then, suddenly, he was gone. No big surprise there.

After that winter, Darryl and his crew were building a rustic restaurant in south Denver. It was about half-framed, and Darryl got his crew lined out with their particular chores. They were building walls flat on the deck. Darryl, with his gentle touch, smacked a familiar butt of the (bent over at the waist) framer. Up popped Billie's grinning face. "I'm working for you," he said. Indeed he was!

I would have fired him on the spot, but he knew that he was rehired before he could drop his tool belt. It was impossible to resist that infectious grin. I can't remember how long this tour of duty lasted, but it was damn sure not a long-term deal.

I think that he went to California and worked for some Hollywood employers, and then he went to climb mountains in the Himalayas. I also heard that he had written a book. Neither this Billie nor any of the others were "just plain Bill."

CHAPTER 9

BIG NOSE GEORGE AND THE FAT CAT

About the middle of the Second World War, Dad decided that we were short of fresh antelope meat. I, of course, dumdummed a bandolier of 06 shells and made sure the proper cleaning and care equipment were on board.

About two o'clock in the morning, the action would begin. All had coffee and bleary eyes but knew exactly where they'd fit in. Rawlins was the first stop. The Paris Café was on the main street of town (US 30). It seems to me that every time we went through Rawlins, we stopped at this old landmark. The front window of the place was an aquarium, and they always had trout of some kind swimming in it. We'd have breakfast, and then, seventeen miles west of Rawlins, we turned north. I don't remember who they were, but I'm certain that we had hunters with us. Everybody wanted to go antelope hunting with Bing! There was never any rhyme or reason to the success or failure of an antelope hunting trip. This trip was one of the difficult kind. We hunted doggedly from daybreak till afternoon and ended up with only one critter.

Most of the Red Desert was open range, but whenever we ran across a ranch house, we stopped and made sure that we were welcome. Out in the middle of nowhere was a ranch house, a barn, corrals, and a little crick. There was no other turn, so we pulled into the yard. Dad and I banged on the door a little bit and heard some stirring—a dog barked and something fell over. We waited patiently for what seemed like forever. Finally, the door opened, and a wrinkled-face, gray-haired old lady grinned at us with that "who the hell are you and what the hell are you doing out here but I'm glad to see you" look. Dad had a way of making people grin.

She was a tough-talking old widow with a gravelly voice and a heart of high carbon steel covering pure gold. Years later, a friend from Rawlins told me that her name was probably Betsy MacIntosh. He said that my description would match her to a T.

Dad offered her a cold drink and with a gesture sent me to our ever-present railway-express cooler. It had beer, ice, melted ice water, and Old Crow whiskey. I looked back for direction and met Dad's glance. "No Crow," he mouthed. Old Betsy had her butcher knife and a big leg of lamb. She sliced off one healthy serving and was starting on the next when a cat jumped up onto the table. The flat side of a butcher knife wielded by Betsy was quicker than the cat's ass, and Kitty-Kitty' smacked the log wall with a double *thump-thump*. Betsy didn't miss a stroke. She went right on slicing sandwich meat for her hungry visitors. Considering her vigor in hitting that cat, I could easily envision the sharp side slicing the cat into halves.

After she had consumed two or three beers and we had consumed several leg-of-lamb and home-baked-bread cat's-ass sandwiches, she told us about her younger life. She had been a tough survivor, outliving a husband or two. After her kids graduated from high school, they never looked back. One comment that she made really impressed me; she said that the last time she was in Rawlins, Big Nose George was being hanged. I think that her memory had slipped a little bit, though, because Big Nose George was hanged in 1881. That would have been around sixty years earlier. She was certainly old enough, but that's a long time to spend in the Great Divide Basin without going to the county seat.

Big Nose George had hung around with the James brothers, and they robbed a train by derailing it. One railroad track foreman just happened by on a hand car and alerted the railroad bulls (or security guards), and two of the bandits were killed. Big Nose George's claim to fame was that the good Doctor Osborne, who eventually became governor of Wyoming, had a pair of shoes made out of Big Nose's hide. Also, Dr. Lillian Nelson, Wyoming's first female doctor, used the top half of his skull for a doorstop.

My dad and I always referred to this old gal as Red Desert Betsy. I don't know about the bandit story, but I can certainly vouch for leg-of-lamb sandwiches and the impressive force of the flat side of a butcher knife.

CHAPTER 10

CARP

One day, this young buck came to my office with his partner and asked if he could subcontract some siding and exterior trim for one of our projects. One was built like a young gorilla and the other was leaner and taller with a constant grin, but did they have any experience? There was no doubt that they had the confidence, but did they know what they were doing? I liked their attitude, so I gave them a shot at one of our buildings. It was of great concern to me that they might screw up a bunch of material that had been purchased by the developer, giving it another reason for a back charge. I waited till they got started before I showed up on the job.

I was impressed with their progress but could see a few impending problems. They willingly listened to my advice and took off like a whirlwind. Everyone was impressed.

I had loaned them some pump-jack scaffold, which includes a device that creeps up a pair of two-by-fours while carrying a plank for workers to walk on, so they could get to the second—and third-floor siding. Carp, whose real name was Paul, was on the high side of the scaffold when he sent his partner, Jimmy, for Coke and stuff. He was busy nailing when a little black kid ran up, grabbed their Skil saw, and ran. Paul didn't waste a second or take the time to climb down. He jumped off his second-floor scaffold and chased the little kid into one of the finished and occupied rental units. He blew through the door, and a big woman said, "What are you doing?" He replied, "I'm after my Skil saw," and she said, "There ain't no Skil saw in here." Paul casually walked over, picked up their TV, said, "There ain't no TV in here, either!" and began to walk out. Magically, a Skil saw was produced, and he set the TV on the ground. Paul didn't worry about any repercussions; he had his saw back and the confidence to handle any situation that came along, even if it became physical.

We planned a trip to Lake McConaughy in Nebraska. Paul loved my boat but had to have a boat of his own, so he bought an old junker from one of his neighbors. We convoyed to the lake and launched the boats.

We had no problem finding the ramp and were set to go, but where?

We had only started my big honker boat when Paul wanted to try his luck on a slalom ski. He made about three tries, and I told him that was enough. He still had the end of the ski rope and started to flounder around. I picked up on his action and wrapped my end of the rope around the end of an oar. When I started to beller about my fish strike, Paul started to act like a giant fish. We had quite an audience before people realized what kind of hoax we were putting on. When Paul was walking ashore, someone yelled out, "Here comes the carp!" Since that prank, all his close friends called him Carp.

In the meantime, my dog Brandy had taken off. Rick stayed with the boat, and Cinder and I went looking for Brandy and a campsite. We stopped on a high point, and Cinder said, "There's Brandy!" I was elated but could not see him in the direction that Cinder was looking. She said, "Right there, playing with Rick." I could hardly see the boat, let alone Rick or Brandy. I thought she was pulling my leg, but my binoculars backed her up. Apparently, her bare eyes were as good as my seven-power glasses. I never questioned her vision again!

We decided that a small cove we had passed would be a good campsite. By the time we got back to the ramp, Paul had his boat unloaded and running. Rick and Brandy drove the Parteaux, *(name of the boat) and Paul followed in his boat to meet us. But he and his junker didn't quite make it to our campsite. He knew that he wouldn't make it and tried for the beach instead. No luck. The boat's windshield was the only thing above the surface of the water at that point. We decided we would deal with this the next day.

Cinder prepared a super meal on the beach, called bami. The only problem was that the blowing Nebraska sand had become an unwanted ingredient. I'm sure our teeth were shinier in the morning, but none of us really gave a damn. We gave the campfire a more than ample dose of water and crapped out.

By morning, Paul's boat looked like the wreck of the Hesperus. Some beneficial soul had pulled it up the beach, above the water line, and removed the bailer plug. No problem! We relaunched Carp's boat, and the engine started, unbelievably. He took it for spin and almost made it back to our campsite before it was swamped again. This guy was so much fun because he could always find something to laugh about.

The next morning, the Nebraska wind was blowing like the mill tailings of hell. No problem! We had pulled Paul's boat out of the water again, and the Parteaux was safely anchored. Then we noticed the waves rolling just past the protective point of our cove. They had miles of reach and were four to six feet high. It was not a good time for boating, but maybe body surfing would be good. How do you body surf? We had no idea, but we found out—it was either body surf or drown!

I had a big, heavy camper on my power wagon and had no intention of getting stuck. From previous experience, I should have known better. Any vehicle in the wrong place at the wrong time can get stuck in the Nebraska blow sand. I was up to my axles and knew better than to dig deeper. When you are in a hole, quit digging. But Carp was driving his macho pickup with humongous tires and wheels. He pulled out a nylon tow rope with a chain and hook on each end. All the towing devices that I had ever seen had been log chains. I had never seen a "snatch rope." After hooking our vehicles together, Carp jumped into his pickup without a word and backed up so that the cars were bumper to bumper. Knowing Carp, I knew there was no time for questions. I got behind my steering wheel, started the engine, and put the car in gear.

Carp took off like a bat out of hell. I knew that his bumper or my bumper was about to become history. He hit the end of his snatch rope, and it stretched about ten feet before my pickup moved. He was almost stopped and burning rubber. I was amazed. There was no neck-snapping jerk, broken rope, or damaged bumper. My car just started moving easily as the rope returned to its original length.

I thought that I knew most everything about getting out of mud holes, snowbanks, and blow sand. Wrong again! This big honyock from Colorado taught a trick to the old kid from Wyoming in the Nebraska blow sand.

Paul was a spectacular athlete and only needed a few sessions to go from water skis to a slalom ski. He glowed all over when he was at the end of a tow rope. I'm not too sure that his little bride wasn't, maybe, a little better. Mitzi had an unbelievable body, a really pretty face, and an amazing sense of balance. She got up on two skis the first time up and then dropped a ski, and she only crashed when she got overconfident, if that was possible. Water skis are not very forgiving. One morning after she crashed, she stepped off the beach on the slalom ski, which involves standing on one foot and waiting for the boat to pull you onto the ski on the other foot. Most water skiers are lucky to accomplish this feat after a year of intensive training.

I thought that my son, Rick, had set the record for moving from water ski to slalom ski, but then Rick was six or eight years younger.

We had a spectacular weekend with fun, freedom, and human relations. After a couple more swampings, we got Carp's boat onto its trailer. We pulled the bailing plug, and it drained water from McConaughy to Strasburg. Then, I never saw it again. In those years that I was trying to regain my youth. Cinder and Carp did a whole bunch to help.

I knew boats—from canoes to rowboats to small outboards and landing craft vessels. Then there are a few ships. It was hard to keep some separated.

We had several new adventures while teaching Jimmy Pinzansham, Paul's partner, to slalom on Carter Lake in Colorado. By the time I had purchased a half dozen permits, the wind had stirred the lake into a frenzy. Jimmy was undaunted; he wanted to learn to slalom. My customary rule was three tries and you're out. But because of the enthusiasm of this guy and his physical condition, I relaxed my hard-and-fast rule. Not only that, but Jimmy was exhibiting some of the most spectacular wrecks that one could imagine. His arms and legs were flailing around so wildly that he looked like a gut-shot albatross. I could hardly believe his stamina and determination, but he finally made a short run on one ski. I didn't have too much trouble convincing Jimmy that we had better leave Carter Lake before we got swamped.

CHAPTER 11

DALE

I couldn't possibly remember all the people who I hired and fired, nursed and cursed, worked with or worked over. Gillette, in the seventies, was the place to be if you were looking for a job. A job to most of these goons was a place to pick up that little piece of paper that converted to greenbacks, which could be converted to a trip to Neverland. The joke of the day was, "How do you get eighteen South Dakotans in a VW? Tell them that there's work in Gillette."

I don't mean that everyone was stupid, but in that time and place, I was probably very fortunate to have anyone who was willing to do anything in the winter of 1978-1979. It was so cold that the lawyers had their hands in their own pockets, and these were tough lawyers.

I had a half decent crew with the help of a renegade type who was a long-time employee and a long-time friend. I'm not sure which one of us was more renegade or why we survived each other. But we've done both, and it's fun to laugh at and with each other.

One day, I was late to the jobsite, but Darryl had the crew lined out. We went to get coffee at the neighboring McDonald's, and he told me that he had hired three new hands. I wasn't too surprised because the head shed had made it plain that we needed all the good employees that we could get. You have to keep hiring until you find out if you got a good one or not.

I had the three new workers in my office trailer, all of them working on their W-2 forms. Big Dale asked if I was from Cheyenne, and I gave him the affirmative. Janice, his sister, asked if I had a shop on Carlson Street and if I had been a contractor in Cheyenne. The pieces started to fall into place. These were the grown-up versions of the infamous prowlers who had challenged, and beaten, every one of my attempts to keep them out of my shop. To this day, I don't know how they entered and escaped, but it seemed that every time I walked through the front door, there was an audible commotion of vermin scurrying around in the separate back portion of my shop.

Their faces sparkled at their realization. They had been the menaces of my shop. They hadn't done any damage, but they had eluded capture for several years. Dale said that those were the best years of their lives. The third new employee, Denise, was a friend of Janice's. She was a little tough looking but otherwise kind of a foxy-looking woman. Early on, she made it pretty clear that she would go to bed with any male of the crew as long as it took place in a bed, not the back seat of a car.

Over the next few days, it became quite obvious that she was after my body. At that point in my life, I was quite content with my sexual life and was not pursuing extra action. Unbeknownst to me, the devil Darryl let the news slip out that, because of my middle age station in life, I had begun using the mysterious potion known as stifferine.

Stifferine, naturally, would change a man into an invincible stud who could polish off one, maybe two, horny girls. Of course, this was a whole bunch of BS.

Denise took this as gospel and was ready for Teddy. I couldn't move around the job site without her huffing and puffing behind me. There had been times in my life that this would have been fun, but this was not one of them. I didn't need more sex! Strange, but true! One particularly cold morning, some of our freeze protection had not survived the night, and I needed muscle. Dale had not shown up the day before, and I hoped he would that day.

The temperature was about fifteen below zero, and ice was forming on the mortar joints of the block work. I had all hands fighting the cold to protect masonry work that had been laid up the day before.

In walked Dale. I gave him a "Where in the hell were you yesterday?" look. He said, "I wasn't the guy who was jumping up and down on the couch in the Holiday Inn. I was the guy who hit the guy who was! Spike (the sheriff) should have said thanks, but he took me to jail!" I had a tough time keeping from laughing but told Dale to get his ass out and help the crew. His antics were fun.

At coffee time, we generally went to the McDonald's next door to my office trailer, where the temperature was about eighty degrees warmer than the outside air. Dale said, "This is the best place in town about five after midnight. They take all the unsold burgers and put them in the trash can in back." A feast! How could I argue? This guy was big enough to eat all the Big Macs in town. Dale had no goals in life. He had been in and out of some of the most prestigious universities, mostly on wrestling scholarships. He could pin a grizzly bear but couldn't, or wouldn't, pass freshman English.

This doesn't mean that he was academically stupid, but it did mean that he really didn't give a damn. I knew all too well about the kids who grew up during the sixties. Even to this day, forty years later, I can pick them out in a crowd. The entire population was somewhat screwed up. The teachers were telling the kids, "Your parents are prejudiced. Black people are downtrodden. Don't trust anybody over thirty." This, of course, was not universally true, but it did have a bad effect on that generation. I'm sure that most of the kids outgrew the attitude, but it temporarily affected a lot of young, healthy minds. Between this and the accepting attitude toward drugs, too many fine young people were destroyed.

Back at the job site, I had made a mistake. The crew that I had hired to pour and finish twelve thousand feet of floor in a supermarket informed me that they couldn't do the job. It required a concrete pumping truck, and I had been able to schedule the pump and ready-mix truck for a Saturday pour. If it didn't happen right then, it would be several weeks before everything could be lined up again.

I called the pumper and told him that I had lost my finishing crew and asked if he knew of any crew that could do the job. He pondered a couple of minutes and said, "It's a long shot, but call a guy named Jim Butler." I called several contractors for referral first, and all of them said something like, "He'll get the job done, but he's always a little scary."

I didn't know how scary till the next morning, when I had concrete trucks ordered back to back for five hours. Jim was there at seven, but he had no crew and was about half popped. He said, "Ralph will be here any minute. He had to drive up from Medicine Bow." Medicine Bow was five or six hours from Gillette.

Ralph showed up about the same time that the first ready-mix truck backed up to the pumper. It was quite obvious that Ralph had had no more sleep than Jim had.

They started the pour!

I questioned my sanity. It reminded me of Julius Caesar's statement that I'd read in high school: "The die is cast. I have crossed the Rubicon." This decision could be a ten- to thirty-thousand-dollar mistake. The die was indeed cast!

These two guys made a Herculean effort just to get that many yards poured. The thing that no one had considered was the fact that Jim's wife would, ordinarily, fall in behind the pour with a forty-two-inch power troweling machine. But with one pissed-off wife and twelve thousand feet of floor that was fast becoming unworkable, Ralph hauled around the discharge end of the pump hose and placed all the concrete. Jim followed and screeded the mud to grade, and then he ran a bull float. About the middle of the pour, Jim stumbled on the mesh reinforcement and crashed to the ground. He sprained a wrist, which made the job that much more impossible. He sat down and drank about three more beers. On an ordinary pour, I always figured that I needed one guy per thousand square feet, and I was far short of that. In desperation, I started to follow Jim with the bull float. By early afternoon, they had started their troweling machines, but it sounded like they were troweling the twenty-year-old interstate. The last six thousand feet didn't turn out too badly, but I knew the early pour was probably lost. I suppose that all people in a supervisory position have made some serious mistakes, but this one looked like a career-ending screwup. I didn't want to think of the cost involved in jack-hammering six thousand square feet of bad concrete. How the hell could I bail my ass out of this one? I called a high-rise superintendent I knew and asked him about pour and grind concrete. I had done a few favors for this guy, and he had no problem with sharing his expertise. His solution was to pour over the bad area with quickset concrete, trowel to the best possible grade, and grind it to as smooth a finish as I wanted. It was certainly worth my best shot. Dale was willing and able, and he was fine with working all alone. I worked with him for a few days just to create some kind of system. It was kind of fun to have someone with more than enough muscle to do the things that were so easy in my youth. Things looked good for a cure to this major error in judgment or bad luck.

Dale plodded on for a month or more doing this tedious work, and we all ended up with an acceptable concrete slab. Done deal, thank God!

CHAPTER 12

DOGS

I've heard different dog owners say, "There's no dog as good as a super mutt." (I use this term only to generalize any owner's boast.) That's true, but you have to define what you want a dog to do.

If you want him to run around yapping, snapping at your heels, and jumping into your arms, there's nothing like a miniature poodle.

If you want a dog to round up cattle, sheep, or other livestock, you'd better not have a poodle or a pit bull because they are going to take a trip to the moon. The ones that you'll love are the shepherds and heelers.

I once heard a guy say that a pit bull could do anything that any other breed could do and then turn around and kick the shit out of the other dog. I said, "Would you like to ask your pit bull to jump into the Platte River, at ten below with ice flows, and retrieve a downed duck or goose? He'd be a shivering mass of muscle in minutes!" Nor would I ask a big smiling bird dog to contest a pit bull.

Which dog is best depends on your point of view.

I love them all but only because of their particular traits. The only dog breed that is offensive to me is a Doberman pinscher. That's because I've never known one that anyone could reach out to pet and be sure that he wasn't going to take a big chomp out of his or her hand. I'd trust a pit bull or a grizzly bear before I'd trust a Doberman. But there are Doberman lovers, and they swear that their dogs are faithful and friendly. I've just never met one like that.

One of the greatest dogs that I have ever known is a cross between a pit bull (American Staffordshire terrier) and a rottweiler. This dog, named Dude, is undoubtedly the most friendly and playful big dog that I know. This doesn't fit the general public's opinion of either breed. Many, many people think of a pit bull as an untrustworthy and vicious dog and the rottweiler as not far behind. I've found that both breeds are great companions and guardians for a loving family. They will not stand for a challenge to themselves or their human family.

We met Dude on our first trip to Alaska. We were with his owners, and he accepted us immediately. His smile is unexcelled. We immediately romped and played with Dude. Considering his ancestry, I don't think that a challenge to our domestic tranquility would have been accepted with any amount of grace. He probably would not be a competitor to a bear, but I'm sure his challenge would run off most other critters. He would at least let us know that there was a threat.

Dude loves to wrestle with his owners and their friends. If he pins someone, he or she is in for a slobbering face wash, and a big grin is usually on his massive countenance. On the contrary, anybody who would offend this dog would be in for a well-deserved ass kicking.

Dude would sit in the front yard of our friend Wayne's house. He was always on a controlling rope for fear that he might challenge one of the bear visitors. I'm sure that a bear would be the only thing that could inflict mortal wounds on Dude mainly because a bear would weigh three to ten times more than Dude.

We wanted to take Dude with us on our fishing excursion, but a two-hundred-pound dog would upset the weight and balance of a nineteen-foot skiff in a significant manner.

Dude was more fun to wrestle with than any critter I have ever contested. He might slobber me to death, but it was always in fun. It was a great pleasure to greet a smiling, huge, fun-loving and challenging bundle of muscle before breakfast. Maybe it wouldn't be a pleasure for most, but for a crazy Kraut, it was a pure delight.

The first dog that I remember was kind of an ugly mutt, and I do mean *mutt*. However, according to my uncle Rudy, Rinky had perfect conformation, perfect demeanor, and unlimited physical talents and would surely take the Top Dog trophy for his breed (a registered Heinz 57 variety American terrier.) He was sired by the best ten dogs in the neighborhood.

His wrinkles were not truly wrinkles but an optical illusion created by the odd coloring of his coat, an unusual configuration of brown and black tiger stripes over his neck and shoulders. He would stand for any amount of indignity from kids of the area, but he was destined to challenge the chow from across the street.

Then there was Tippy. He was probably the prettiest and dumbest dog that we ever had. We took him pheasant hunting one fall, and once was enough. After running through a few weed patches, all of his beautiful golden hair was impacted with cockleburs. On the way home, he rode in the back of the pickup. It had a nice cover and a mattress, but the cockleburs were chewing him up and he was chewing up the mattress. The cockleburs adhered to the stuffing in the mattress, so when we got home and opened the tailgate, a giant jumped out. I think that there was very little of the stuffing that was not carried out on our great hunting dog. It took hours to shear the poor critter. He also had a bad habit of chasing the light reflections from the windshields of passing cars. He was pretty lucky because he lived a charmed life in spite of chasing reflections.

We had a German shorthair pointer that was a super hunter. It was delightful to see her running full bore and then catch the scent of a bird. She would fly into a classy pointing position and land without tumbling head over heels. She would always get her limit of birds, but she really didn't care whether it was a legal rooster or an illegal hen or the farmer's laying hens.

CHAPTER 13

HORACE

Horace is one of most interesting people I have ever known. I'd heard tales of his adventures and activities from the time I was old enough to be awed by anything. He was a man among men. He did things in the natural course of his life that the greatest adventurers would write novels about. He was one of my heroes.

It made no difference if you were an orphaned kid, a monkey, a rooster, a raccoon, or a cur dog. If you *really* needed a home, you were welcome at Horace's house. He was not, by any means, the tender, loving, psalm-singing sister that might be conjured in your mind. Horace was probably the toughest man that I ever knew, but he had a respect for life and the living that is all too missing in the world today. He probably made the mistakes in life that we all do, but people knew real quick if he thought they were wrong.

I'll never forget the story about a calf-roping horse that had pushed his patience a bit too far. The horse was obviously plumb dumb. Horace decided that too much was too much and grabbed the chin strap of the nonlearning critter. He gave him one punch in the snout, and the horse dropped like a rock, either learning a lesson or becoming the entrée du jour at the local fox farm.

My dad hired Horace to move a house from downtown to the east part of Cheyenne. I was amazed at the feat. In less than a week, the house was moved onto a foundation that Horace had laid up. I think that this guy could do anything that he set his mind to.

The next time our life paths crossed, Pappy and I were building a house for a young couple east of Cheyenne when Horace stopped by. He said that he had some time on his hands and would give us a bid on the brick veneer. He gave us a good price and did a good job, but these were only two of the benefits of his presence on the job.

Two of his younger boys provided a constant karate, kung fu, jujitsu, cowboy, or alley fighting display that was unequalled. At that site, all the topsoil from the lot was in one pile waiting to be spread in the appropriate areas. These two young bucks had climbed up and fought their way down so many times that all an excavator had to do was smooth it out. It was already spread!

Another time, I was in the office of the most knowledgeable and competent construction performance bond expert, Bill Murray. Bill had provided Horace with a bid to demolish a smokestack at the University of Wyoming. A kind of reprobate, retired Marine had it all planned—a couple of strategically placed sticks of dynamite would make quick work of the structure. All Horace would have to do was scoop it up and sell it for used brick and solid fill. No problem! Except there was a problem. The job specifications required that all material be dropped inside the stack and hauled away. Bill had underbid the job by enough to make any bondsman nervous. Horace said, "I found out how the generalissimo beat me. It's only fifty stories; he's going to thread it and screw it down!"

Horace always had big pen of hounds. The only ones that I remember were greyhounds, mostly for running coyotes. At this particular point in time, he must have also had some coon hounds because he had a young coon on a chain with a doghouse for weather protection. I don't know whether a coon needs that, but this one had it. Directly above this young coon was a small monkey that ran back and forth on the clothesline. A coon is a good climber, but not on a steel clothesline pole.

The monkey would hang by a leg or its tail a smack the coon in the kisser. It was something to behold. The monkey knew that if the coon got a hold on him, he would be history.

I was the successful bidder on a building for Guy, Phelan, White and Mulvaney—four of the few attorneys that I thought that I could really trust. To be included in this contract was the clearing of the lot where the new building would be built. I hired Horace for this portion of the work. He came in with the necessary equipment to remove the big old cottonwood trees. After he had cut them down, the lot was pretty well covered with trunks, limbs, and branches to be sawed up, loaded, and hauled off. I came upon this scrambled mess at about coffee time and poured Horace a cup from my thermos. His two boys were fighting, as usual, and one of them picked up a broadax and looked like he could whip the world. Not to be defeated this easily, the other tough kid grabbed a chain saw and gave the cord a couple of jerks. Horace bellered, "Knock it off, you damn fool kids, before you ruin something!" Needless to say, those two honyocks grew up to be as tough as Horace without a fear in the world.

No matter the circumstance, there was never more action than what Horace created. He was always a great man to know.

CHAPTER 14

A FEW BLACK FRIENDS

About the only black guys who were our age when we were growing up were from the Rhone family. I knew the two boys near my age, but one was two years older and the other was two years younger. I got to meet their dad at the lumberyard where I was working. I was only fifteen years old, but the manager left me in charge while he was gone to lunch and the regular yard foreman was on vacation. It was usually very quiet during the lunch hour, but one noon hour a very big and pleasant-looking black man walked in the door. He asked if Mr. Singer, the manager, was there. I said, "No, but he will be back soon. Can I help you?" He asked my name, and after I told him, he asked if Bing was my dad. When I said yes, he gave a great big smile and said, "Everybody in town knows Bing." He said, "I'm Buck Rhone. Maybe you know some of my kids." "Sure do," I replied. About that time, Max Singer returned and took over my relationship with Buck.

A public park in Cheyenne was named for Buck. His older son was a legislator in Colorado for years, and Tommy, his younger son, became a very instrumental figure in education. They were good people.

Buck's fist looked to be the size of a small ham. He had been a promising heavyweight boxer in his younger days. His participation in this profession stopped immediately when he was booked to fight

King Kong Kelley. Buck was smart enough to realize that his time was up and retired to a more stable profession.

I met "Big Ed" at the same lumberyard a couple of years later. A different owner had me on his records and offered me a short-term job unloading a carload of sacked cement (ninety-four pounds each). Ed and I unloaded that car of cement and sort of began a friendship. I didn't see Ed again until a couple years later when I was a carpenter apprentice and Ed was with the same lumberyard. We renewed our friendship, and Ed did a bunch of unloading for me that he wasn't required to do. One Christmas, Ed took me to his favorite bar, which had strictly black patronage and a scary history during WWII. I would never have gone into this establishment alone.

But I had no problem going with Big Ed. I have never laughed more in my life than I did there. The bartender was not very big, but when a drunken patron challenged him, a big revolver magically appeared from under his apron. This would-be troublemaker was looking down the barrel of a very nasty looking gat. It was a really interesting experience, but I don't need any replays. I was always very content to be a friend of Big Ed's.

The two Geralds could have been twins. Although they were seven hundred miles apart, both were tinners, or HVAC (heating, ventilation, and air conditioning) repairmen. Both were good, honest employees. The one in Las Vegas worked for an Italian ex-hood who had somehow became a heating and air-conditioning contractor despite not knowing shit from applesauce. He threatened to drop a quarter on me (use an untraceable pay phone to call a mob hit man) several times but said he didn't want to waste a marker on a nonpaying Kraut.

He had a son-in-law who worked for a very legitimate company, and his daughter was a hard-working gal who had to be the brains of the company.

Gerald was big and overweight, and his boss dropped him off at the house project that we were working on. The temperature got well over one hundred degrees every day, with no shade in sight. It was miserable! A little after noon, Gerald started cursing the bastard he was working for. He said, "Don't that man know that if one of us black guys get too hot, we *explode*!" Gerald was big and strong and was always willing to help do the muscle work for any other tradesman on the job.

The other Gerald was strikingly similar to the guy in Vegas. About the only time I saw him or was around him was at a coffee break or lunch. His work attitude was so positive that he was well worth his salary just by being on the project. Whenever someone would start raising hell or just pissing and moaning, big Gerald would comment, "It's not so *baaaad*!" He said the final word in an unreal high-pitched falsetto voice. Coming from a man as big as Gerald, that immediately brightened the mood of every man within earshot. A personality like this on any job is worth a fortune. Every guy on the job would smile when Gerald walked by.

When I was in Las Vegas, I worked with four black friends almost every day. Two of them worked at the security gate at McCarran International Airport. One was a lady who was always pleasant and smiling, but it would take a gorilla to give her any contest. Lucky was a smaller man who was fun to be around anytime. One day he would be very cordial, and the next day he would mock a tough, mean, overly strict security guard. He always kept me on my toes and had the authority to do whatever he threatened. Most of the time, he was just practicing. If we had to bend the rules, he was the first one we would talk to.

One day his partner let it slip that his birthday was that day. We went to the nearest liquor store and bought a mini bottle of Chivas Regal scotch and a pint of milk. During his duty, we presented our birthday present. Booze at the guard station was strictly forbidden, but Lucky was pleased that someone really cared. He threatened severe punishment, and we all had a good laugh. He was indeed an exceptional friend.

One year, my two granddaughters spent a few days with us, and I took them to the airport to catch a plane home. The departure time was within minutes, the big DC-10 was loading, and I kissed my two darlings good-bye. But

one of the big engines refused to start, and the flight was canceled until another plane arrived from California.

The airline offered to buy all the passengers lunch at a nearby casino, and my two granddaughters made a smart decision. They found an airport security cop and told him that I worked at the airport. He called the security control office, and they radioed me. I was there in minutes and found that my friend had taken good care of them. Every time I saw him after that incident, we reminded each other of his rescue.

I worked very closely with the airport authority locksmith. George was a well-educated, skilled man. Whenever I installed a lock, I was required to give George the keys, and he would give me the combination to program into it if it was that type of lock. George loved a joke, and we would swap stories any time we crossed paths. Sometimes I would want to get into an area that was restricted by the airport authority. If I didn't have a key or the combination, I joked with him that if he wouldn't give me access, I would change the combination to all the airline break rooms. He grinned and offered, "You do that, and I will have the authority change the combination on *you*." 'Nuff said.

CHAPTER 15

GOOD COPS, BAD COPS

Johnny Crock was about the first cop I remember who had any reputation one way or the other. We pretty well looked up to this man, who was a long-time member of the Cheyenne Police Department. Seeing this guy on his motorcycle assured that no crime or hanky-panky went on while he was around. The only time that he got after me was when I was being stupid. I had a carload of kids in my little red truck and drove through the homecoming snake parade.

It was quite an awakening when I got to the other side and looked at Johnny on his motorcycle face to face. He didn't do anything except give me the "stupid kid" routine in front of all my classmates. He was a good cop. The next summer, I was driving home for lunch and came to a barrier in the street that was keeping people from driving in the fresh oil tack coat. Foolishly, I decided to drive on the wrong side of the street to stay off the fresh oil. Right after I got to my house, a cop by the name of (we'll say) Ed Pinhead pulled up. He gave me a ticket and then told the judge that I had driven on the wrong side just so I could drive on the fresh oil. That lying SOB was a bad cop.

The summer after we had moved to Gillette, Cinder and I went fishing with her new resident fishing license. We had caught a nice bunch of DeSmet rainbows and enjoyed them with great satisfaction.

A couple of weeks later, two game wardens came to the door and started asking questions. I think Cinder had probably told them about our good luck at Lake DeSmet. Then they started asking questions about a bunch of other stuff. Pretty quickly, Cinder said, "Am I in trouble for something?" They said, "Yes, ma'am. We are going to give you a ticket for lying about your residency in Wyoming."

One thing that really pissed her off was to have her honesty questioned. The trial was set for a week or two later, and the two officers had to make another hundred mile trip to attend. Cinder took a couple of receipts for the rent for my room and board from well over a year ago. The judge asked, "Is he the head of household?" She replied, "Yes," and the judge banged his gavel and said, "Case dismissed!" So two officers had traveled four hundred miles and hours out of state for one stupid ticket. They probably cost the State of Wyoming hundreds of dollars. It was not good.

I had another incident with one of the same officers. I had my boating license but had forgotten to attach it to the boat. My son and some of his friends had come up to visit and go fishing. I told the officer this, but he said, "Every time you hit the beach, I'll give you another ticket!" I'm sure it was all perfectly legal, but he cost me five hours of travel and pretty well messed up the fishing trip with my son. Slobovian cop!

Another time, my grandson and I were fishing at Glendo State Park on a beautiful day in July when two game wardens who were driving a party boat gave me a ticket for not having a Coast Guard-approved throw pillow which is a cushion with straps used as a device for swimmers in trouble. These two goons made me follow them a couple of miles back to our campsite to be safely equipped while a big bunch of drunk partiers were tearing up the lake on Sea-Doos, water toys, and overpowered boats. I asked them, "What about those guys?"

This asshole had the gall to say, "We can't catch these guys who are not from Wyoming."

I asked my lawyer granddaughter what a Philadelphia lawyer was, and she answered, "About like a Slobovian game warden."

I began to have a bad outlook on game wardens, but most Wyoming law officers are the cream of the crop. I just had the misfortune of finding a few exceptions.

When we lived in Gillette, I got to know a dirt contractor very well. He had several deputy sheriff friends. I think he had been to law officer school with them.

Greg loved trapshooting. We went to the local trapshoot club together and practiced a little. After we shot a few rounds, he asked me if I would fill out his team. I didn't think twice about it and told him I'd love to. He and I were the only two on the team who were not deputy sheriffs for Spike Hladky, the famous sheriff of Campbell County. I could write another book if only I knew some of the things that this superman did for justice in Campbell County. Some of the tales were purely Old West style.

Spike's deputy sheriffs were completely professional. All had been to FBI school and had gone through any other training that could improve their skills. I'm sure that being Spike's deputy entailed more training than any other law enforcement position.

We lived in the country and were one of the few houses in our development. We finally agreed to let our teenage kids have a party one night. We stood watch over the bunch, and I do mean bunch. All went well, and some of the kids stayed around long enough to clean up all the beer cans.I hadn't thought to tell my deputy buddies about the party, but one of them had watched the whole affair. They had known about it the whole time. They were some of the best. These guys could handle any trouble that came up and somehow knew where trouble could happen. I have no greater respect for any man than this type of lawman.

The year that I spent shooting with these guys was better than any year of sports that I remember. We won the division that we were in, and Greg bought silver trophy buckles, one of which I have worn ever since.

These guys knew the difference between good and bad. They had handled everything from stupid misdemeanors to the worst that any boomtown ever could offer, and they did it with exemplary professionalism. These were the top of the order as far as I am concerned—good cops.

After we had moved to Powell, my son, an old employee, and I started building a house on the 160 acres of my dreams. The foundation was done, and we needed all the material to frame and close our new home. I had a list of materials already called into Billings, and my old 1971 power wagon and a twenty-foot trailer were ready. It took me all day to go to the various lumberyards and supply houses. It was hot, and I was sweaty and thirsty. I stopped in a little town in Montana just north of the Wyoming border and bought a six pack even though I never liked to drink a can or a bottle of beer. I always liked it poured into a glass.

I stopped in a convenient spot just before I got into Wyoming to check my load and tighten straps here and there. Satisfied that my load was secure, I cracked open a can of beer and began leisurely pouring it into my glass. All of a sudden, I felt something looking over my shoulder. I looked up, and there at my window was a Montana State Trooper. I looked him in the eye and said, "I can't believe that you watched me do that!" I think he was biting his lip to keep from laughing, and he asked, "Is everything secure?" I nodded, and he said, "Okay. Drive carefully."

Really good cop!

CHAPTER 16

CPA

CPA stands for Certified Public Accountant or maybe Champion Pal Always. Either one would describe my friend Johnny Bath.

I had known all the other Bath brothers and sisters before I met Johnny. We had all spent summer holidays at Guernsey Lake. The boating and water fun was secondary to the friendship shared around the campfire on the beach.

Johnny was different from his brothers and sisters, and for that matter, everyone else that I ever knew. They had all grown up as ranch kids, and not one had wanted to run a ranch. There was probably enough land for several ranch operations, but all the kids wanted to live in town. Johnny was the only one to follow a profession.

He and I became acquainted in Denver. Rex, my partner at the time, knew that Johnny had moved to Denver and that we were looking for an accountant. We talked with Johnny a little and decided he was our man. We had tried various ways of beating income taxes, and Johnny just laughed and said, "All you guys are doing is making the lawyers and accountants rich! If you make good money, smile and pay your tax!" That's not to say that he wouldn't use every line of the tax code to save us money, but he knew exactly what would fly and what wouldn't. I'm sure that more than one IRS agent spent sleepless nights trying to figure out what had happened. Johnny's logical interpretations of lawmakers' wording was almost always contrary to the apparent intent.

One year I got audited and called Johnny. He called the IRS and made an appointment to give them what they wanted. He brought all my books and records, and we met at the Hampden Street office building. It was a real experience to observe the different expressions, body language, and especially the attitudes that Johnny took on when we walked into the IRS office. He was the CPA version of George Foreman. I could see him, in my mind, sparring, shadowboxing, feinting, and knockout punching prior to the fight. We gave the receptionist our names and appointment card. We didn't have to wait long. When our auditor showed up, she was one of the foxiest, classiest-looking chicks that either one of us had seen in a while—and wearing a miniskirt. She introduced herself and asked us to follow her to a little office cubicle. Johnny and I were both divorced at the time and had exercised our critical eye on a good number of Denver area ladies. This one was among the finest (looking, that is).

She had to have taken five years of postgraduate bitch courses. She questioned every major entry in my books and asked for receipts for proof. At one point, she said, "This check that you have written to the University of Wyoming may not have been for your son's tuition. It may have just been for cash." I have never seen a volcano erupt, but I have seen Johnny Bath erupt. The big book—I don't know if it was the ledger or a journal, but it was about three feet across—was spread out in Johnny's lap. With no countdown, Johnnie jumped to his feet, slammed the book shut with a tremendous WHOP! and said, "We have shown you every receipt, every check, every deposit! You question a man who is honest enough to keep his personal gas tickets separate from his business gas tickets! *You prove us wrong!*"

The mouth of Miss Beauty Queen Bitch looked like a trash can with the lid off.

As we were walking out, with every eye on the whole IRS floor looking at us, Johnnie said, very casually and quietly, "Pink, if the tax due notice is less than two hundred dollars, pay it." It was, and I did.

Times were good. We were both newly divorced, and we had plenty of money.

There were girls, ladies, chicks, and a few broads. If you were divorced and had money and a little class, the world was your oyster My biggest problem was the fact that I already knew the lady I wanted to share my life with.

Johnny and I spent lots of hours laughing at, and with, the world. We met a couple of gals at a PWP singles dance and arranged a double date for the following weekend. John's date was a brassy, scoundrel kind of broad. After dinner, we went to a local lounge at somebody's recommendation. Our waitress served our drinks and was taking orders at an adjoining table when I noticed a fiendish look on the face of Johnny's date. The waitress squealed and turned around as if she were going to smack a molester, but there was nobody there. Miss Scoundrel had a telescoping pointer and had run the point of it up the waitress's leg. Then, she quite deftly retracted the pointer into a tool about the size of a pencil. The poor victim looked bewildered and did her best to regain her composure. A few minutes later, the same waitress was placing an order at the bar station. Out came the telescoping pointer and up between the waitress's legs it went. Scoundrel struck again!

Johnny was very good at analyzing human situations. We took his advice and left at the first appropriate chance.

After I had married Cinder and went to Gillette, I got a notice from the IRS that an error existed on my 1978 tax return and that I owed three hundred and some-odd dollars. I called Johnny, and he told me to send him the notice, which I did right away. About a week later, he called and said, "Hell, Pink, if that's the way they want to play, send them the money. We'll win!" I had no idea what he meant, but I sent the check.

I had completely forgotten about this little deal when I got an envelope from the Treasury of the United States. It looked like a check through the envelope window. Sure enough, it was a check, and it was for seventeen hundred beautiful US of A greenbacks.

I paid them three hundred dollars, Johnny filed an amended return, and they sent me a check for seventeen hundred dollars! I always hoped that Miss IRS (Denver examiner) was the one who was scratching her head about that one. I signed one of my best IRS returns with only the knowledge that Johnny Bath had prepared it. It was for the fiscal year of 1977 Rick and I had tried to build a framing crew for the work that we had contracted. We had two possible workers, but every other one we hired seemed to deserve firing. I can't remember how many we went through, but it was a bunch. The feds were trying to curb the effects of the recession of the time. In order to do this, all employers were encouraged to hire new people with promises of receiving a "job tax credit." Part of each new employee's income tax, for wages up to forty-five hundred dollars, would be credited to the employer. Some of our new hires didn't even make forty-five bucks before they were fired. Our mantra was, "Do what you're told, do what you think, or be willing to do something." If none of these worked for someone, he or she was history. Johnny was particularly stressed that year and left a message for me to come and sign the return, but no payment was required. He was gone to Mexico.

I called Johnny after he got back and told him that I was really glad that I had no tax to pay. He replied, in his false, high-pitched, exasperated tone of voice, "You don't even know the good news?" I didn't, but I did know that it wasn't going to be long before I knew the 'good news.'

I waited just long enough to piss him off and then asked, "What news?"

"Pink! Big Unc owes you nine grand!"

I went to Johnny's office the next morning and became convinced that it was true. My next stop was the Loveland Airport where an airline pilot had a Skylane for sale. I flew this bird around the patch a little, and the seller checked the compression. I was a little suspicious of the fact that his air tank ran out before we had a holding pressure on the number six cylinder. If I had pressed this issue a little, I might have had a less expensive repair bill. Airplane traders are no different than used car traders or horse traders. I bought N9387X anyway.

In about 1980, both Johnny and I were pretty newly remarried. Things were going well, and a little vacation sounded even better. I called John, and we decided that a trip to Lake Tahoe was just what we needed. Cinder and I would fly to Laramie, pick up Johnny and Judy, and then fly on to Lake Tahoe.

Things were set. We left Gillette in clear weather, but most of the trip was above the clouds and Cinder was not too thrilled. We got near Laramie, and I called their flight service station. They gave me airport conditions and the active runway. As soon as we got into the landing pattern, I discovered that the air speed indicator showed nothing. This was not a real biggie but definitely an inconvenience. We later found an insect nest in the pitot tube (the airspeed sending unit) and cleared it.

Johnny and Judy were there on time, and we were on the way.

Cindy and Judy fell asleep in the back seat. Johnny had some flying experience and helped with the navigation. We put in enough *uh-oh*s and *oops*es to get the gals' attention, but they pretty much slept through the whole flight.

I had planned on a fuel stop at Wendover. The chart showed only a small airport operation, and that's just what it proved to be. The deceiving factor was that this airport had been a bomber training base in the WW II era, so the runways were arranged in a triangle to facilitate landings or take-offs in any wind condition.

They were all a hundred feet wide but were not all maintained. We taxied to the fixed-base operator and tied down. The airport was a ghost town. The forties vintage barracks were still all there but were in bad disrepair, with windows broken out, windblown roofing, and peeling paint. The base operator came out and topped off our plane. We asked if there was a taxi available, and he said, "Sure! About five minutes at the front door." Five minutes later, there was our taxi. We got in to find that the base operator was driving the taxi! We went into Wendover, had lunch, gambled a little, and caught our taxi back to the airport. Some jewelry in the store caught Judy's eye, and she asked our base operator/taxi driver if there was a sales clerk around. He pulled his cap off, brushed his hair back, and said, "What can I help you with?" This guy was the whole deal.

I did the preflight checks while the gals were climbing aboard. We were set for the rest of the trip. As I was about to start heading toward the run-up area when Johnny grabbed my arm and, with great authority, pointed to a sign that said, "Please Don't Take Off from the Tie-Down Area." There was enough concrete in almost every direction to make a standard takeoff. I gave him my most professional nod and taxied to the end of the runway. It was a hot afternoon on the desert, and I was glad that we had all that concrete in front of and below us. Even a Skylane with a full fuel tank and four passengers has to work a little to get airborne.

We crossed over Reno and were soon over Lake Tahoe. It has to be one of the most beautiful lakes in the world. We were maybe two thousand feet above the surface, and it looked like we could see two thousand feet into the lake. While Johnny and the gals were oohing and aahing, I was wishing that I had studied the approach charts a little better. My only approach plan was to simply fly down the lake and land the plane up in the valley facing uphill. My radio contact had advised that the active runway was just the opposite. I was to fly up the valley, turn toward the base, and land down the valley—downhill. When you're landing on a downhill runway, the plane has a tendency to keep flying.

Suddenly the oohing and aahing stopped. I was flying as directed, but it looked like we were headed straight into the mountain (and we were). Johnny looked at me and suddenly realized that I had my hands full. I turned right base to final to align with the runway. Suddenly, an old instructor comment came to mind: "You can't dive to a landing!" I pulled full flaps and put my plane into a slip. From all outward appearances, we were in a dive. PMP (point of maximum pucker) for all! Actually, the plane was in controlled (I hoped), uncoordinated flight. We dropped like a rock but didn't gain speed. A good, firm *bump-bump* confirmed that we were on the runway.

A few minutes later, Johnny relieved all of our tension. After we hit the airport bar, with the signature JB facial expression, he said, "The best scotch I ever tasted."

We laughed, played, gambled, and had a good flight home.

Life was good!

CHAPTER 17

DARRYL

I can't remember how or where I met this challenger, employee, partner, friend-to-the-end, problem-from-the-start, fight-if-you-want guy. Without going further, you must know that our great relationship has not been an easy road. There have been bumps.

My early training was purely union. Darryl had learned the trade from a whole bunch of derelicts who were not all bad but only cared about the piece work price. A combination of both would be the best of all worlds.

I think that Darryl had not been very happy with his employer and was looking for another job. We had two projects going and needed a whole new crew for the latest contract. Somehow, Darryl showed up and had the dubious credentials of running work for our current bad-ass competitor.

For one reason or another, the conversation kept creeping back to Darryl's crew. It became quite obvious that Darryl *and* his crew would come to work for us but only as Darryl and crew. I had never hired such a bad bunch of derelicts, but somehow I had confidence in my decision.

I was somewhat disturbed by the unorthodox proceedings of this crew but decided to stand back and watch for a while. They displayed very little that would match my way of building, but things were happening. Most of our other crews built things the way I told them. If I told Darryl how to do something, he would just stare at me with a blank look and go ahead with his way.

It was somewhat exasperating because he was getting things done. It didn't take long for me to figure out that I had a renegade crew to deal with, but I was wise enough to keep these guys on the payroll.

I had a super tough Native American named Manolito who didn't seem to fit with any other crew, so I sent him down to Darryl's crew. He worked there almost half a day before Charlie Martinez, the backup carpenter (and one of the best employees that I ever had), called me aside and said, "Buenger, you'd better get Manolito to some other job!" I asked, "Why?"

He said, "Mano can't stand Darryl! At coffee break, he threw his framing ax, and it stuck in a two-by-four about two inches in front of Darryl's face!"

They were two good employees, and I didn't need either one to be killed or be a killer.

The next morning I took Mano out to help me on the house that I was building for my family. I haven't had many full-blooded Native Americans as employees, but the ones I have had were the best to work with on a shoulder-to-shoulder basis. There seemed to always be a problem with their accepting "white eyes" ways, but this only gave me more respect for their truly honest heritage.

We always left the hiring and firing up to the foreman or superintendent who was running the job, but we did take individual cases into consideration. My secretary, Jeannie, was a great help. She was one of the best "people" people that I've had the privilege to know, let alone employ.

She was not a grandmother type but, somehow, knew each individual for his or her own traits. Every person on our payroll somehow knew Jeannie. She took care of them like an old mother hen. Jeannie was as cool and pretty as Barbara Mandrell. Sometimes I wonder why I didn't steal her.

Every guy who lasted on Darryl's crew was a renegade of some sort. His brother hung around for a while, and there was Crawdad. A really strange one was a kid from Cheyenne who had gone to high school with my daughter. He had lots of brains and talent but was overly impressed with the misinformed, civil rights-twisted attitude of the sixties.

Billy was a renegade from the start. I think that he was a "job site hire," but those were generally the best kind. Billy always wanted to be on the top floor as a building went up. It wasn't long before he was experienced enough to set the roof trusses, place the backing, sheath the roof, and look forward to another. The amount of help governed the timing. I don't remember any other employee who cherished the "top out" more than Billie. Our guys got somewhat overconfident with handling materials. We did have the best machinery that was available. Among these behemoths was a Pettibone Super 6, a forklift that could lift a bunk of plywood thirty-three feet and place it gently on the roof if the operator was skilled and the guy on the roof would guide it into place. It was somewhat scary to know that one guy could make the difference between a properly placed load and a tipped-over forklift. Needless to say the forklift operator would lift this kind of load only to an experienced and trusted guy at the top. We rented several forklifts, borrowed a couple, and bought two Super 6s. In six years of multifamily construction, we only crashed two of them.

The work dried up in 1975, and Darryl left for greener pastures—Gillette, Wyoming. Some of his crew followed, including Crawdad, Curley, and Grizz. I never was a macho-fighter guy, but for some reasons the troops would not challenge me. Maybe they thought that I was not far away from an "equalizer." I'll never know, but I do know that I had only one employee threaten to kill me.

Darryl had a crew put together to do some of the subcontract work in Gillette. At that time there, roughnecks (oil field workers) were making a thousand to fifteen hundred dollars a week. Any one of our crew would be gone in a New York second if he could get on with a drilling crew. But it took a hell of a tough kid to stay on with these drilling crews. Fortunately, their records went with them. If they didn't last long on one crew, they wouldn't be hired on the next.

We got the rejects, and most of them wouldn't last through one payroll period. Dogs were a dime a dozen.

Darryl was not a kind man to his crew. They either worked hard and fit in or they were gone.

We had a contract with a commercial developer to do the interior framing and trim for a new grocery chain. As usual, our planning and projections were being screwed up by an incompetent superintendent. I got a call from the ivory tower saying that our work was not up to par. I wasted no time in calling the general superintendent to tell him about the incompetent supervision of the project. It was make or break time!

I got a call from the owner of the company the next morning. Bill Grace was about as direct as anyone I have ever known. With him, it was either black or white. We both spoke our own minds in a matter of seconds. This started a good relationship.

Bill said, "You do what you're contracted to do when the timing is right. You don't need to worry about anything else!" We'd struck a chord! From that moment on, the timing started to be right.

For several months, I had great pleasure in flying my own bird (N-9387X. a Cessna 182), back and forth from Denver to Gillette and being able to write it off for expenses.

The superintendent's name was Bradshaw. He claimed to be an uncle of Terry Bradshaw (the Steelers quarterback). It made no difference. Sports are sports; business is business. Darryl saw a challenge for both teams. His ever-present challenge to the world was a given.

Chapter 18

Horses and Mules

The first horse that I could really appreciate was half draft horse and half saddle horse. She belonged to an old rancher in the Beaver Creek Valley with whom I had spent a few summers. Her name was Punk, and she was pretty much an all-around mare. Anybody could ride her, or she would work under the harness in an emergency. I could catch her anytime with a bucket of oats or a handful of cake. The only problem was that she was always in the bog, a pasture that was flooded with groundwater. She had foaled a few times and had a naturally fat belly. I was free to take her for a ride anywhere on Flohr's land or into the Forest Service land. I never got lost because all I had to do was give Punk her head and she would take me home

Quite often, I would ride her while dreaming and gazing around without any idea of where I had wandered to. After I would look around for landmarks and find nothing familiar, I knew it was time to let Punk take me home. More than once, when I finally recognized some landscape, I realized that I was a long way from where I thought I was.

The neighboring rancher had a nice-looking bay gelding with a bald face that I thought that I needed. I seldom needed a horse in my young years, but my dad liked this gelding too, so it was easy to convince him to buy the critter. This kind of started the horse craze in our family. This horse's name was Buttons, and my dad became so fond of him that he bought me a fifteen-hand sorrel gelding that was pretty classy looking but wasn't much good for anything but pleasure riding or show. Rube was as gentle as a dog and could be caught anywhere with nothing more than a carrot. Sometimes we rode him without even a halter. This ability gave rise to many a prank pulled by someone on the ground. Rube would take his rider for a trip without anything to hang onto but his mane. One day, my friend Mid jumped onto old Rube and went for a ride. I knew Rube would come back by the pickup, so I hid behind it. Sure enough, Rube came running by the pickup, and I was ready. Just before they passed it, I jumped out and bellered out a big, "Yeah!" Old Rube took to the air, and Mid came flying right out in front of me. I was laughing so hard that I didn't see Mid coming toward me. I got a Sunday punch, and that was the second time that Mid broke my nose.

Dad later found a really classy-looking three-year-old, mostly thoroughbred gelding that came with a house deal. We went over to take this critter home, and of course I was elected to ride him out to Dad's friend's little ranch. I guess that I was pretty lucky to get

Sox clear out to Chris's scatter without some kind of bad event. We didn't handle Sox for about two weeks and found out that a daily workout was pretty necessary for any green-broke colt.

I had planned to ride Sox across town to Dad's pasture on the south side. Chris had a good round corral, and we didn't have much trouble getting a bridle on Sox. I walked him around the corral a few times and put my roping saddle on him. No problem, but that was my first mistake. Then I opened the corral gate and led Sox out (second mistake).

I turned Sox in a few circles and casually stepped into the stirrup without anyone nearby (third mistake). As I swung my leg over, Sox jumped forward and I sat down in back of the saddle. Sox was not a strong bucker, but any rider whose ass was not in the saddle and feet were not in the stirrups had a predetermined fate. Sox ran about three strides and went ballistic. I flew off and landed on my head. My neck has never been the same.

We called an old cowboy, and he showed me how to straddle without landing behind the saddle. I had to adjust the reins in my left hand and grab the headstall, and with my other hand I held the stirrup, got my foot in it, and then grabbed the horn. Then, if the bronc jumped, I could pull his head around. I could ride pretty well with his head pulled around, my foot in the stirrup, and my right hand on the horn. Good lesson!

At some point, Dad bought an Arab mare for my mom. This little mare was as pretty as a picture but a little too high-spirited for my mom. She was not too bad unless someone tried to ride double, and then she was pure trouble. We took Queeny elk hunting one year. She wouldn't leave our old faithful, Spot, whom we had hobbled, and neither would the rest of our horses. We made her the bell mare, which means that we hung a cowbell on her so we could find our horses in the morning. We all fixed our bedrolls around the fire and crapped out. One of our party from Rock Springs had pulled the oats sack under his head for a pillow. Queeny smelled the oats, came near, and pulled the sack from under Mark's head. He woke up and was sure that Queeny was a bear. He squalled loud enough to be heard for miles. Queeny broke and ran right through the campfire, bucking, snorting, and kicking our fire all over the place. It took a while to get settled in again, but nothing was hurt.

Then I thought I wanted to compete as a calf roper, so I bought an old has-been buckskin. I don't think that anybody had a rope long enough to catch a calf with this horse. I'd get on the calf, and as soon as I twirled the rope one time, Buck would slow up. He's the one that fell on my left leg and screwed up that knee forever. I took him elk hunting one year and tied red flags all over him because he was the same color as an elk. I probably would have been better off if I had let somebody shoot the son of a bitch.

We bought a palomino that a friend had used as a registered stallion. The problem with him was that he didn't sire any palominos, so our friend castrated him and sold him to us pretty cheap. He was really pretty—pretty worthless and pretty apt to stay that way.

A real horseman friend of ours had a jet-black horse that named Croppy. His ears were clearly cropped. He was a mean-looking critter because he always looked like he had his ears laid back and wanted to do somebody some bodily harm. My friend's brother Henry had had one too many incidents in which Croppy would rear up and go over backward. The last time that Croppy did this with Henry, Henry jumped on his head while he was down. Croppy's name had been Jet before this incident, but his name was Croppy after Henry let him up.

Walter always liked Croppy and took him off of Henry's hands. Cutting his ears off didn't cure Croppy from this nasty habit. Each time Walter would first put the saddle on, he would step into the stirrup and put his weight on as if he were about to climb on. Every time, Croppy would perform his stupid stunt, and Walter would step off and let him crash to the ground. After Croppy's performance, Walter would say Croppy was the best horse he ever had. You had to be a cowboy like Walter to live long and do well with a screwed-up critter like this. Another trick of Walter's was to go elk hunting and take only the tack and a horse trailer. He would head for his hunting area, keep his eye open for some horses along the way, stop and borrow a horse for his trip, and then bring him back after he was done. Only Walter could pull this off because horse thieves were often shot or hanged in Wyoming.

I worked on a ranch on the Little Laramie River. At that time, the livestock was fed with a team and a sled. One wintry day, the ranch hand who fed the bull pasture didn't show up, so I got the unwelcome chore of feeding this herd. There were not too many bulls, so this pasture also put up a string of mares and a quarter horse stud. I had my sled pitched full of hay and pulled away from the stack. No sooner had I lined my team out and climbed up to pitch the feed in a windrow than I saw this stud horse sneaking toward my team. He looked like the Pink Panther on his tiptoes. The son of a bitch got to my team before I could get down.

He was biting, pawing, and squealing right in the middle of my team. A smack on the ass didn't faze him, so I stabbed his ass with my pitchfork. It took me about half an hour to calm my team enough to untangle the mess. Luckily, I was able to unhook the tugs and straighten out the whole smearcase. I wasn't a bit sorry for stabbing that ornery critter, but I also didn't want the high-dollar stud to get an infection.

The last horses that I owned were a bunch of sale barn losers. I knew it when I bought them, but they served the purpose at the time. One strawberry roan was a well-bred, well-trained, good-looking animal. I wondered why I had been able to buy him so cheap. It was soon very obvious—he was a cripple of sorts.

His conformation was so perfect that his front feet were not conspicuous. They were so trim and well-shaped that no one would suspect that they were just not big enough to carry the weight. He was always footsore. Buying a horse is a challenge to beat the odds, but very few really win on all counts. One tidbit is that you should never buy a horse that has been branded seven times! If a horse is in the livestock sale barn, it's a pretty sure bet that someone plans to cheat and someone is going to be cheated. I cheated someone myself a few years later in the Billings sale barn. Life goes on!

CHAPTER 19

NATE BROWN

Our granddaughter Sarah spent a summer with us. She loved horses and really needed a horse that she could control. My previous attempts had proven unsuccessful.

We looked at some fox-trotters that would have been perfect, but they were beyond my budget. We both loved one in particular and his fox-trotter gait, but I didn't have a horse that could keep up with his fox-trot. I would have really been thrilled to buy this horse, but that would have meant another thousand dollars to get a mount for myself.

We went out to another recommended horseman. He was such a BSer that he had a special little gazebo-type building for the sole purpose of spinning his yarns. We weren't too impressed with his overpriced horses but enjoyed his horseshit and gunsmoke tales.

He spun a tale about the biggest rattlesnake, which had struck his boot top and left fang marks. I commented, "That was a pretty big buzz worm," and he replied, "Yeah, considering that I was riding a fifteen-hand horse."

Soon thereafter, an ad in the paper caught my eye. Apparently an old horseman was selling off his collection of horses that he had provided for the Girl Scout camps in the Bighorn Mountains. I called the number and was assured that I could buy the right horse for Sarah. This guy's place was down by Meteetsee, about an hour's drive. Sarah, of course, was excited about the possibilities.

We took off the next morning with my horse trailer in tow. Nate's scatter was so typical of cowboys' homes. As we pulled into his yard, we almost ran over him. He was obviously an old bronc stomper. His legs were so bowed that he wouldn't have been able to stop a hog in a ditch. He tipped up his hat and displayed a face that would be pretty on any woman. His eyes were ocean blue, and he had a smile that matched their sparkle.

He had a short conversation with Sarah and said, "Let's go look!"

Nate had a horse in mind. He led us to a corral full of horses, and I was a little disturbed by the difficulty he had in catching Becky. She was a light-boned bay mare that was not happy with the new deal. Nate put a bridle and saddle on her, and she offered no resistance. Sarah knew what "leg up" meant and was there in a minute.

This little mare knew it all. She had been used as a cutting horse, a roping horse, and a barrel-racing horse, and she was plumb bored with Girl Scouts who knew nothing about performance.

Nate tied a bailing twine around the chin strap and walked Becky with Sarah riding for a couple of rounds in the corral. He pulled the twine from under Becky's bridle, and Sarah was riding a horse that could do what she wanted. Nate said, "Kick her." Sarah gave the mare a little kick in the ribs, and Becky started a gentle trot. Sarah's face lit up like Christmas tree. It was quite obvious that Becky had been a competition animal in her earlier years. I bought the critter and took her home to our little scatter in Powell.

For the rest of that summer, Becky taught Sarah to appreciate the virtues of a true usable horse. Becky was never easy to catch or really gentle to handle, but she made any rider sit up and pay attention to his or her riding. Becky somehow knew whom she would tolerate. A tough little neighbor wanted to ride her, and Becky didn't go fifty feet before she blew up and threw this little girl onto the Wyoming sod. I'm quite sure that Becky had dumped some Girl Scouts in the same manner. Horse personalities and girl personalities needed to match somehow. I don't have a clue how old Nate knew how to match the girl to the horse.

Sarah and I went for a little ride into our "habitat" pasture, and Sarah kicked Becky into a full-blown run. About two rounds later, they were headed back to me, but the drainage crick was between us. I wanted to cover my eyes because I knew that there was a humongous leap or a bad wreck in store for my granddaughter. Becky didn't look twice and jumped the dry wash! Sarah lost her seat but pulled herself back into the saddle. I sighed a giant breath, and Sarah grinned from ear to ear.

Becky took Sarah from wannabe to horse rider in about six weeks. Those were some of the most delightful times of my life!

CHAPTER 20

MY NATIVE AMERICAN FRIENDS AND EMPLOYEES

Before I was of school age, my family moved to a small house in West Cheyenne. All the neighbors were pretty much average people of the time. The only fault was that we were only a few blocks from the railroad tracks.

This was right in the middle of the Great Depression, and there were hobo jungles all along the tracks. Our next-door neighbors were a small Native American family. Their son Jimmy was a year or two younger than I, but we became pretty close friends. Jimmy's mom, Ruby, was from the Oglala Sioux reservation and was the daughter of a Sioux chief, which made Jimmy pretty aware of his heritage. His dad, Rock, was not around much.

One day, my dad came home when Jimmy was playing in the street, and Dad told Jimmy that he had better play somewhere else. Jimmy took great offense to this and said, "I'll cut your eyes out and eat them for dinner." Jimmy obviously had gotten some coaching from somewhere.

One evening a few years later, our doorbell rang, and my brother-in-law went to answer it. A caped figure stood by the door and screeched, "I am the phantom!" These kinds of antics were the norm as long as I lived anywhere near Jimmy.

A couple of years later, we moved to a much better neighborhood and school. The next year, Jimmy moved too, and we were in the same school. Jimmy's mom had a crippled leg and was always pretty angry at the world. They moved around often, but Jimmy always kept in touch. When he was fourteen, he called me and said he had just graduated from Air Force paratrooper school. We saw each other a couple of times after that, and he would get in touch, either through my sister or a mutual friend, every five or ten years until he died in California. I think that I was the only "white eyes" that ever really understood him: he was an Oglala Sioux chief's grandson.

At one point, I had been working for my dad for a couple of years, and he gave me full supervision of a really complicated apartment complex job. At that particular time, I had no experienced help. I called the Wyoming employment office, and they had only one available hand who would come close to filling my requirements. They asked me if I had any problem if the guy didn't have transportation, meaning that I would have to pick him up and take him home every workday. This was not a big problem, and then they told me that he was a Sioux Indian. As far as I was concerned, the cowboy and Indian days were over, so I told them that was fine. They said that his name was Paul Victor Yellow Cloud and that I should pick him up at Snug Harbor at eight o'clock the next morning.

The Snug Harbor was a cheap boarding house for transients and was not necessarily bug proof. It reminded me of the words to "King of the Road": "Two hours of pushing broom bought an eight by ten four bit room." Nevertheless, I picked him up the next morning. I found that he didn't speak very good English, but with some effort and a few hand signs, we got along pretty well. I wanted to get the high work done first, so we started the morning building scaffold. I asked him what I should call him—Paul, Victor, or Yellow Cloud. He shrugged his shoulders, so I said, "Chief!" He grinned and nodded his head. Done deal.

One fall morning that year, it was especially cold. Chief was glad to have the work and to be able to save his money. He started lecturing me, saying "Winter coming. Buy long underwear, buy overshoes, buy warm coat, and pay for room." I said, "You wise Indian. Now climb up here and help me snap guide lines." I had laid out the spacing that was needed and told him to hold the end of the chalk line on the marks. Then I gave him the chalking and unreeled the chalk box to my end. I pulled it tight and snapped the chalk on the wall. Chief was really impressed and called my chalk box a "box full of lines." He asked where to buy such a box. I'm sure that after he got back home, the Sioux reservation had red lines snapped everywhere. He was a hard worker, and I had to be sure that I told him when to stop shoveling or he would move a mountain.

I mentioned earlier that I hired a slightly built Native American in Denver, whom we called Manolito. He was always good to work with if he was with the right crew. When he threw his hand axe and narrowly missed his foreman's head, it became necessary to find him a new crew. Manolito's brother also worked for us for a while with no trouble. They both came to work one day, and we told them that it was too cold so they should come back around ten. They went to a nearby bar with a couple of macho jocks on our crew. Things erupted, and they tangled. Thankfully, no one was hurt very badly.

Years later, I hired a young Native American in Gillette, just outside the Sioux reservation in South Dakota. His name was Gary Pellitier, and he was smart, young, strong, and athletic with a good attitude. We were building a steel building at the time, and I also had a steel worker working in his off-season. This guy was very experienced, and Gary learned very quickly from him. I had visions of him becoming as good as he looked. This steelworker could walk up a steel I-column with no kind of ladder, and Gary would be right behind him.

I had a franchise with a major manufacturer and was hoping that Gary was good enough to lead a steel building crew. Sadly, this was not so. One Friday night (payday) Gary went out drinking. He and booze were not a good mix at all, and he got into a fight with some super macho coal miners. They were apparently showing how stupid they were, got Gary down on the ground, and proceeded to kick him enough to teach him a lesson. He came to work the following Monday morning but was hurt too badly to do anything. I never saw him again. If I had known who those goons were, I would have hired Grizz and Dale to give them a little cowboy justice or blow them away and let them lay in the gutter where they belonged. I have often thought that I should have followed up and prosecuted those bastards. I don't know when this kind of injustice will ever cease for the once proud and self-sufficient people.

CHAPTER 21

JAKES

My dad had friends who were mostly of the top order, along with a few derelicts along the way, just for spice. Jess Jacobsen, or Jake, was one of those on the top end. One of the best adventures of my life was with this Sarwegian not only a Sarwegian—he bane a Dane! Jake worked for United Airlines as an A and P (air frame and power plant) mechanic. In the thirties and forties, Cheyenne was the main maintenance depot for United Airlines. Cheyenne is a thousand feet higher than Denver, but the Rocky Mountains give way to the Great Divide Basin. The Continental Divide is a hundred miles wide in the basin but doesn't climb to the thirteen- and fourteen-thousand-feet level as it does in Northern Wyoming and most of Colorado. The prejet airplanes that spawned air travel, like the Ford Trimotor and the DC-3, simply could not safely and efficiently climb to these altitudes. Jake was one of the few A and P mechanics to make the transition from carburetion to jet power. But then, Jake was Jake!

Dad, Jake and I were determined to find—or refind—Firebox Lake. Dad and Jake had both been there before, but neither one was sure of the true location. This small lake in the Snowy Range of Wyoming was the source of some strange tales from the American Indian.

We were driving a famous 1936 Dodge pickup, and the distance downhill wasn't too scary, unless you considered making the same trip back up the hill in mud. Luckily, we found the mysterious lake. Dad didn't like boats and especially disliked rickety rafts, but Jake wanted to show me the firebox for which the lake was named. We paddled an abandoned log raft over some strange-looking water to the edge of the firebox. There appeared to be schools of fish, but they spooked at our raft and disappeared into the depth of the hole. It was almost like gazing at space through a telescope, only in reverse. There appeared to be no bottom to this crystal-clear lake. We didn't spend much time there because of the feeling that it might gobble us up. We didn't catch any fish in the lake, which made us think that the fish we saw were not really there at all. We did manage to catch a bunch of brookies in a nearby crick.

By the time we got back to the pickup, the skies had clabbered up and spilled a small torrent of water. The road back up the hill was like goose grease. We fought our way for fifty or sixty feet and finally decided to go for help. Dad and I headed up the hill toward a lumber camp, and Jake said he would work some at getting a little more distance up the road. We walked maybe a mile up and another two miles to the timber-cutting camp. A big Swede was enjoying a beer on his front porch. He grinned as we walked up, with that experienced expression of a man who'd spent his life in timber country and knew that the road that we were walking on was the very reason that we were walking. A summer rain would make little rivers out of the two tracks and make them pretty impassable for a few hours or days. He asked us into his home and introduced us to his wife and two daughters. Teenage Swedish girls are generally, in my humble opinion, honestly prettier than any movie queen there ever was. Sven had no problem loaning us a big dapple-iron gray mare that he used mostly as a skid horse.

The big old mare walked quietly into her stall, and we got the collar and harness on with little complaint. The only problem with draft horses is their slow gait. If you don't like the first speed, you damn sure won't like the other one. It took us about an hour and a half to get back to Jake and the pickup. I couldn't really believe the progress that he had made all alone. We hitched the skid horse whiffletree to the pickup bumper, and big old dapple-iron Babe walked up the mountain with our pickup in tow, never breaking a sweat.

My association with Jake was on and off on for a good many years, although he had to move first to Denver and then to California in order to stay with his profession. I'm pretty sure that a good number of United Airlines jet mechanics still maintains the standards that Jess Jacobsen lived by. Jake became a shirttail relative of mine through a couple of marriages. I was brother-in-law to Allen Jacobsen, who, along with his brother, bought a shoe repair store in Laramie with their GI Bill money. I think the original name of the store was John and Jakes, if I remember correctly. Although Jake was a few years older than me, we got along well and did some great trout fishing with Pappy.

During this time, my dad died of leukemia, and I was wandering and wondering where to go next. I spent a month or two at the Union Pacific switching yard and maybe a month at the alumina plant in Laramie, when I stayed at Allen Jake's house. Allen was always ready to help a friend. One of his customers was a tough old cowboy who was ramrodding a big spread of ranches for Miller Brothers, a Jewish origination that ran everything from cow-calf ranches through yearlings, strays, and horses to a sale commission yard in Denver.

I'm proud to be an uncle of Gary Jake. I have known this Jacobsen since his birth. He was always grinning about something. Sometimes a guy might think that he knew something that everybody else didn't know. I kind of lost track of him till he was around twenty-five. He had become the cowboy that he was destined to be and, really, always had been. He was a college-educated cowboy with the practical, hard-work experience and knowledge that's required to be a true cattleman. Somehow, we communicated shortly after I had married Cinder. He was on a ranch near Lusk, Wyoming. In talking with Gary Jake, I found out that he had fed a few critters and that we might be able to buy half a cow. I had just married Cinder, and the appetites of our three teenagers were healthy. A few weekends later, Cinder and I drove down to the scatter that he was ranching.

It was a real experience for Cinder, and I learned a few things that were only in the dreams of the most advanced cattlemen when I was cowboying. Along with his ranch foreman job, Gary Jake was allowed to run his own herd. The day that we were there, he was sorting and penning his herd. He had around two hundred head of Charlet cows and no bulls. He artificially inseminated his whole cow herd and was getting an unusually large calf crop. Cinder asked some questions that Gary Jake grinned and answered but that would have driven most cattlemen under the sanctity of their hats.

In the last few years, my history of accidents and illnesses seemed to rub off onto Gary. Horses are always a great source of accidents. Gary Jake was riding across the river last year and had no clue of an impending wreck. When he reached the near shore, his saddle horse made the expected lunge to clear the river bank. How was he to know that his drivers were on top of a beaver run? The river bottom collapsed, the saddle horse went over backward, and Gary Jake caught the stars. In the end, he had a dislocated shoulder. It's always nice to have an honest horse that will put up with whatever contortions you have to go through to get horseback again just to get home. Gravity isn't easy, but it's the law.

Within a year of that incident, Gary Jake's appendix decided to burst just before calving season. After running all over central Wyoming, he was bound and determined to find a doctor—or die. He put a heavy load on the medical staff. "It's calving time!" he said. "I gotta be back in the saddle within a week!" They did whatever it took, and he got back in the saddle in time.

When Cinder and I were in Las Vegas, Gary Jake and his wife Cheryl came down for the National Finals Rodeo and looked us up. This was a special treat because a whole bunch of the world figured that we were down and out. We were damn sure down but were not out! Somehow, Gary Jake knew it.

He and I were discussing our bad habits—his chew and my smoking. In an effort for both of us to quit, we shook hands on a bet of a hundred bucks. I was able to quit but had forgotten about the bet by the time I did.

Several years later, things had turned around for me. I retired and returned to Cheyenne to build a house for Cinder and me. One night, I gave Gary Jake a call, and he invited me out for dinner. He told me to come an hour or two early so he could show me his cattle operation. This was a cool break from my house building. He moved seventeen hundred head of cattle simply by moving the salt lick sled, whistling, and getting his dog to round up the stragglers. His method was a hell of a lot easier than the time-honored, lightning-quick, cow-smart but rough-riding quarter horse.

On the way back to dinner, Gary Jake said, "Ya son of a gun! Ya beat me!" I had no idea what he meant. As soon as we pulled into the yard, he handed me a C-note. I must have had a pretty big question mark on my homely face. He explained that I had quit smoking but he hadn't quit chewin'. I'd triple my payoff if he would shitcan that snuff in his pocket.

It's a commonly known fact that girls from the East are a little bit cautious because they think that worn circle in a cowboy's Levi's comes from a condom container. Maybe they quit chewing tobacco, but they keep carrying the can.

Gary Jake has that quick wit that cowboys are famous for. We'll still be friends after bad habits have claimed us both.

CHAPTER 22

THE HAT

My generation was not particularly attracted to the hat, and it seemed that none of us had matured enough to be comfortable with the many styles of hats that our dads had worn. As a matter of fact, we used to refer to a hat as a "man hat." I guess that we all had hats of one description or another but hadn't gathered enough sophistication to feel comfortable with them. Even today, I see all these macho men running around coaching football teams, reporting the latest news and weather, and doing all kinds of outdoor sports with nothing on their heads—all but Tom Landry, who always wore a hat. One of the most important survival facts is that the greatest amount of body heat is lost through the head. I keep thinking that these guys standing out in hurricane-force winds and rain with nothing on their heads must get carted away, suffering from hypothermia.

Back to my story. Cindy and I were in Las Vegas at the height of "lifus mos miserabilus." Sam's Town's tent sale was at its peak of activity. All Western clothing, tack, and footwear was offered at close-out prices.

I was telling Cinder about the hat that I had talked my friend Bob Stager into buying at last year's sale. Bob was a man of big stature and an appropriate job (he headed the Bureau of Land Management's wild horse program), and he needed a hat to match. We had walked by the Stetson hat booth and saw a hat of enormous proportions. It was jet black with a Montana crown, Hoss creases—like those on the hat of Hoss from *Bonanza*—a five-inch brim, and the pencil roll. It had been special ordered by a very important man or a magnanimous BSer. It was a twenty-five X beaver felt hat and had an interior band imprinted with the store name: Tejas. I was somewhat concerned at Bob's response when I took it off the display head and smacked it onto his bare head. The salesgal gasped with delight (or superb salesmanship). I told Bob that he looked like a British Jew from Lubbock, Texas. The gal fell into mock-swoon, and the high-dollar, special-order hat was bought for twenty-nine dollars. Bob wore it regularly for several months, and then it was obviously missing. We were BSing in Bob's tack room, and I noticed the big Hoss hat hanging from a handy splinter with a half-moon chunk missing from the brim. Bob answered my question before I asked it: "Melba's mustang!" Melba was a neighbor gal who had adopted one of the desert mustangs. Bob had thrown his big hat over a corral post, and Melba's mustang had bitten the chunk out.

Bob was completely bummed out about the whole thing and told me that it would cost him ninety bucks to have Stetson repair the brim. I said, "Bob, you can see the individual teeth marks from this savage critter. Can you imagine the tales that you might spin a about the character of your hat? That hat's worth a million bucks! You ought to wear it everywhere, but if you don't, put it in a display case!" Bob smiled at the thought.

The hat sale that year when I went with Cinder was equally spectacular. The salesman took one look at me and said, "I've got a hat that's perfect for you!" When he pulled down a Hollywood Pearl, five-inch brim, Roy Rogers-style hat, I began to have serious questions. He and his assistant began their style preparation with great vigor. They steamed, rolled, ironed, and caressed this special hat. Cinder and I had wandered some distance when the foxy little assistant came running. "Sir! Sir!" she hollered. "Come try on your hat!" She had visions that this multi-X, silver beaver hat would turn me into a rhinestone cowboy. I never was and never will be that dashing, daring, handsome cowboy that is supposed to be under a hat with the Roy Rogers crown. No doubt, though, it was of the highest quality and styled to perfection—a thing of beauty.

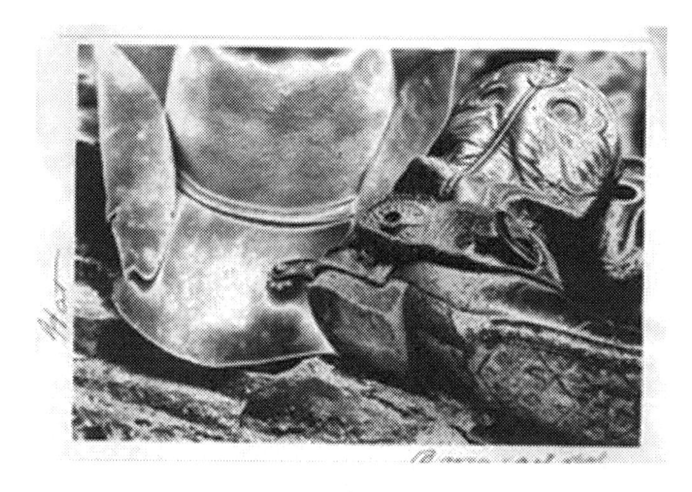

With great apprehension, I crammed this long, oval-shaped, size 7 1/8 movie-star hat onto my sauerkraut square head. (We learn very early that a square peg doesn't fit in a round hole.) I could feel strange things happening. All the styling on this side of hell couldn't have prevented the inevitable. The classic brim rippled like a Hawaiian surfer wave, and the crown resembled a pile of road apples. I'm damn sure glad that my male ego is well suppressed by my sense of humor. The hat salesman, my wife, and the foxy assistant broke into uncontrolled laughter. The salesman pointed at a mirror, and I directed my glance to see the hilarious transformation. It could only get funnier. I gave it my best country bumpkin face, and Red Skelton would have been proud of me. I removed the damn thing immediately. If it doesn't take him to the bank, a guy can't stand to be laughed at forever. The salesman regained his composure and said, "I apologize for the outburst, but I've been selling hats for twenty-two years and I've never seen a hat explode like that. We'll find you another one." I declined. As we walked away, I made a radical decision: I wanted that G-D hat! For $21.99, I could have a silver-belly, five-X beaver, umpteen hundred dollar hat. It may never be seen outside of my fishing boat, but it could be used as a good sunscreen or maybe something to stomp on when I lost a good fish or a handy fabric on which to wipe anything that I may need to wipe. I went back and bought it, and it still brings chuckles from those who know the history.

CHAPTER 23

DUCK SOUP

Cinder and I had moved to the Bighorn Basin, bought 160 acres, and built a new home before we had any idea that the national economy was headed for the worst recession since 1929. The first indications were becoming apparent; our tenants in Gillette were starting to go broke.

We were trying our best to hedge against Brokesville ourselves. I had accumulated a lot of construction equipment and had no good use for it. An auction generally brought about ten cents on the dollar for such equipment, so we decided that a rental store might just be successful in Powell. We didn't rush into it without doing some research, and it looked very possible. We ventured into Powell Rental. Things started out pretty well, and we were being accepted by the community.

One morning, an old Mormon gentleman walked into our little store. He inquired about a tandem wheel trailer that I had built, originally, to move to Gillette. We gave him our rental rate, and he asked for the rate on my old Dodge pickup to pull the trailer. We hadn't set a price for it but pulled a price out of the air. Then, he looked at me and said, "How much for you?" We all laughed, and I told him that he had better see what I could do before he agreed on a price. He told me that he would be back right after lunch if I'd have everything ready. Sure enough, he was there at the stroke of one o'clock.

I had no idea what he wanted to haul on the trailer but soon found out. We went a few miles west of Powell, and he said he had sold this farm but had to get his storage building to his place south of town. The storage building that he wanted to move was about ten feet wide and eighteen feet long. "How are you going to get it loaded?" he asked. I noticed that there was a strong emphasis on *you*.

I backed the trailer into position and pulled out my handyman jack. If I put it in the middle of the building, the trailer would not be able to get underneath. Old Brigham offered his own handyman jack so we had one for each side. About the time that we got the little building high enough, my old pickup started rolling back. (The emergency brake wasn't very good.) The trailer knocked the jacks out of the way and kept rolling till the building was teetering over the end of the trailer. There was not a damn thing that I could have done, so I went on as if this was just another common chore. The old kid's eyes were in a state of disbelief—mine too, if the truth were known. I pulled out my hand winch, winched the building onto the trailer, boomed it down, and said "Where to?"

Our destination was only about five miles away, and we made it in no time. Brigham had a very tidy retirement farm and had already staked out the exact spot where he wanted the building. I put the trailer over the spot, hooked one end of the chain to the building and the other to a good, solid fence post, and then pulled the trailer out from under the building. I knew that the building would be bent in spots if it dropped off the end of the trailer, so when there was about three feet of it left on the trailer, I stopped and released the hitch on the pickup. The building was pushing the trailer and would not release. I figured that, when it did, it would jamb the tongue into my tailgate. I was on a roll. I shifted the pickup into compound low, raced the engine, and dropped my foot off the clutch. As soon as the gear grabbed, it jerked the hitch loose, the trailer dropped its tail, and the building slid to the ground without the slightest bump. Brigham pulled out his billfold and said, "You're worth as much as the truck and trailer," paying me twice the price that I had quoted him. He dusted off his hands and said, "Duck soup!"

CHAPTER 24

PAT THE THIEF

Shortly after my partner Rex and I parted ways, my son Rick and I were doing enough contracting to keep the wolf away from the door. We were hiring and firing on a daily basis in search of a crew that would make more returns than we had to pay them. Sometimes, we had to cut a little slack to a promising new employee. This was the case for a particular individual that Rick liked. This guy was built like a yearling bull, had an infectious smile, and looked like he really wanted to do something. Rick hired him.

Pat really kind of stumbled around, looking for something to move, pound on, stand up, or maybe even build. It didn't take long before we realized that Pat wanted to do something and he didn't care what. He never balked at anything that we asked him to do. I think that if we had *ordered* him to do something, though, he would have been gone in a second.

We had finished one project and started on another. This developer was no smarter than the rest. His house foundations were inaccurate, out of square, and the product of a screwed-over, underpaid concrete contractor. We were not much different, but knew going in the intentions of our employer.

Pat learned quickly and soon had tools for his new trade, probably the spoils of a neighboring builder.

Our crew almost looked like it knew what it was doing. We hired a goofy-looking goon to fill Pat's former laborer position. Pat really liked our confidence and was committed to being a good framer. One morning, we had a garage wall ready to stand up and drop over the bolts. This particular wall was twenty-five or thirty feet long, and we had enough crew to raise it without undo strain for anyone. For one reason or another, the wall didn't match the drilled holes in the bottom plate, and the crew was balancing it on top of the anchor bolts. I dropped to my knees to see which direction to move it. I had barely hit the ground for a look underneath, reaching for the wall for balance, when it decided to settle onto the foundation. The thumb on my left hand was pinned between the bottom plate of the wall and the concrete foundation. Only a big hammer can mash a thumb as flat as this. I might have said a few words of damnation, but I really didn't have to. The whole crew knew that I was a stationary fixture until somebody lifted the wall. Pat had just used the wrecking bar and knew exactly where it was. In a matter of seconds, he had the wall lifted enough to free my mashed thumb.

I didn't have to worry about getting the usual purple nail that results from blood under the thumbnail; the wall had avoided this problem easily. Blood was spurting out from under my nail. It was coffee time anyway, and several of the crew provided ice to pack my flat thumb in. To this day, my left thumbnail is a lot wider and flatter than the right one.

One hot summer day, we were taking our morning break in the foyer of a luxury home that was finished as far as our crew was concerned. The idle conversation came around to Pat's family history. Pat had mentioned his dad before but never very specifically. I asked Pat what his dad did for a living. Without hesitation, he said, "He's a thief. I'm a thief. My uncles are all thieves!"

I had to think a bit before I responded, "Why in the hell did you answer our ad in the paper?" He said, "I never had a job before, but Rick said we paid every Monday morning. I never had a sure payday! We always had to do some muscle work or arguing." We did, in fact, pay every Monday. If we had paid on Friday, we probably would not have had a crew on Monday morning.

Pat was a good hand and stayed with us longer than most. Thief that he was, I never had any concern that he would steal anything from us. As a matter of fact, I'm sure that Pat would have administered some street justice to anyone with that intent.

Pat always enjoyed a prank. Rick and I worked hard at finding a laugh at anybody's expense, and Pat was no different. We knew to never laugh at him—always *with* him. Construction is hard work, and the hours went by more quickly if we could look back and see what we had accomplished while having fun. Pat enjoyed the honest, hard work that Rick and I provided. He fell into the work-a-day life and an honest paycheck.

A couple months after we had finished that project and laid off all of our employees, Pat called me and said he had a five-year-old pickup that he would sell for five hundred dollars, with a clear title.

I thought about this deal for maybe a half hour and decided that the only way that this could happen would be if he had been wasted. At that point in my life, I didn't need any more problems! However, we did need a 327 small-block Chevy for our Gillette employee Darryl. I mentioned this to Pat. Two days later, he called me back and gave me a number to call. This guy sounded a little shady, but I didn't expect much more. I drove down to his house, and he was very cordial. He invited me in and offered a cool one. It was a little disconcerting to see a Thompson submachine gun hanging on his fireplace wall.

I mentioned Gillette, and my newfound acquaintance said, "I'll be damned. My woman has opened a 'massage parlor' on North 59." I knew that this business would thrive in Gillette if it weren't for the tough-as-nails sheriff but made no comment.

After a few quaffs of his cool one, he said, "Let me show you that 327."

We went out to his yard, and he already had the engine sitting on blocks. He asked, "Do you want to hear it run?" "Okay," I said. "Why not?"

In a matter of seconds, he had a battery, gas can, and tie downs. The engine looked like it had been taken out of a brand new wreck. I said, "Okay, I'll buy it for $250."

Then he offered me a 383 Dodge engine that he had to get rid of quickly. I figured my old pickup could use a heart transplant, and it sounded like he was a little desperate to get this engine off his property. We started it, and it sounded fine. He said, "Two bills," and I replied, "No, but I'll give a hundred." Done deal! I left with my two engines before the police got there. Sometimes you have to be quick.

Darryl put his little engine into a boat. I was really surprised at the performance because I never did like Chevy engines. Most of the time, they started and ran with plenty of torque, but I had never been able to get one to run very long. As far as I know, that engine ran as long as Darryl's "boat mode" lasted.

I've had a lot of interesting employees, all with their own particular traits, but this self-admitted—and maybe proud—thief was one who personified "honor among thieves." I'd hate to think that I fit into the same category, but there was never a question in my mind that Pat would not steal anything from me.

Maybe Rick and I had a positive effect on his life. I hope so.

CHAPTER 25

PERRY

"You fired who?" I was asking a big question, the answer to which troubled me deeply. Bobby Calhoun, who had been with me since his apprenticeship and had been a big part of any success in my professional career, had just fired the best framer that either of us had ever seen. I thought, *Holy shit! This guy never takes more than one swing at a sixteen-penny nail.* This was a spectacular ability in the world of rough-framing carpenters. Not only that, but he had a bag of tricks that could only have been acquired through an extraordinary interest and desire to be the best. I had ultimate faith in Calhoun's decisions, but this one would take some time to digest. At that moment, I didn't want to talk about it and decided that I'd better let that rabbit sit.

I walked down to our saw yard and stumbled onto the realization that my partner Rex had been in trouble for several days on Black Hawk, one of our other projects, and had taken the Birdman, our premium forklift operator and prefab man.

How much horseshit can a man put up with in an hour and a half?

It was plain to see that we were not hurting at that point, but all I knew was that a crew of twenty-five or thirty framers had better use up a lot of building material or we'd all be in trouble.

Bobby didn't go into any reasons for firing Ben, and I didn't ask. At the coffee break, I noticed a certain improvement in the crew members' attitudes. By lunch, the productivity was definitely better. *Ding-ding* goes my brain! *Does the fact that Calhoun fired Ben Vigil have something to do with this?* Bobby told me later that Ben was one of the best that he had ever seen but that his "God-like" mannerisms were screwing up the whole crew. Sure enough, the morale on the job site took a giant leap, including in Ben's younger brother. Apparently everyone realized that if Ben Vigil could get fired, attitude was as big of a factor as ability. This was all great, but I didn't want to fill in as sawyer on a permanent basis—an entirely different problem but still one that needed to be resolved.

A VW bus pulled up into the muddy mess of a nearby building, and a slightly built young hippie jumped out with a determined look on his face. He questioned the first guy he met and was directed to me. Without hesitation, he marched directly toward me. I liked his determined look but wasn't too impressed with his stature. Our average framer had long hair, lean and mean thirteen-inch biceps, and a size two hat. Some were overeducated, and some would never be. All would flip the peace sign but didn't necessarily know what it meant. This young man appeared to be mature enough to trust someone over thirty.

His opening statement was, "Sir, I need a job. I'll work hard, and I'm no dummy." It occurred to me that these words were not much different from my own when I got my first break in the building industry.

"We'll give you a try!" I said. "Come back tomorrow morning before seven. We work seven to three-thirty, half an hour for lunch and a couple of coffee breaks. Okay?" "Yes, sir!" he said, his face lighting up. It's always a pleasure to find a young man who wants to work instead of those guys who have to.

The next morning, Perry was at the job site before I got there. Bobby Calhoun had the crew lined out, and Perry was glad to see me drive in. The saw yard looked like a ghost town. I didn't need to talk with Bobby about the cutting list until I had some idea that this new employee could handle the job. Perry had just lived a wild goose chase and was definitely in the mood to work an honest day for an honest wage.

At the first coffee break, I asked Perry how he had ended up in Denver. It was a long story of a dream going down the tube. He and his wife had left a prestigious university back East with the promise of an unlimited career in medical research in South America. He got to Atlanta and called his benefactor, who immediately told him that the salary would be reduced considerably. Before he crossed the border to Mexico, he called again and found out that the job could only provide him and his wife room and board. Busted dream! Thank God for the VW bus. They were short on cash to start with, but things were getting critical. Perry told me that he had asked for a job at every place on the way to California and then to Denver. I began to realize his plight. I could tell that he was working on determination, not groceries. At three thirty, quitting time, I asked him if he could use an advance on wages. "Yes, sir!" he said. I could see the accounting going through his head as he accepted the twenty dollar bill—mostly to feed him and his wife and fuel his trusty VW bus. It doesn't take a psychiatrist to figure out that this kind of young man would be a trusted employee. Within a couple of weeks, he had my whole cutting list and prefab program memorized and was working on improvements. Ordinarily, a common framer would be jealous of such a rapid advance in authority, but this guy was welcomed by all. They didn't realize how quickly he had mastered his newfound trade. They all thought that Perry had come to the job with this ability. They were right, to a point. He had come to the job with ability but gained the knowledge because of his enthusiasm and desire to succeed.

It was pretty obvious to me that Perry would not be a long-time employee, but he stayed with us until we finished the first phase of Highline Meadows. There was no doubt in my mind that Perry and his young bride had stashed every extra dime to ensure their success in their future. Perry had lived up to his original statement, and we rewarded him with good wages. It was plain to see, however, that as good as he was, construction was not in his future. We shook hands when he left, and I had the feeling that he was destined to make the world a better place.

About a year or two after Perry left, I got a letter from him. He had found a job in New England, and his employers were so impressed with him that they put him in charge of one of their branches in Europe. He thanked me profusely for his job and made it pretty clear that the twenty-dollar bill I had advanced him had kept him from going to a soup kitchen. Now he was well on his way to leadership in his career. I think he knew that he had not only bailed his own butt out but had also saved me a whole bunch of time in finding an employee to handle the job that he learned so quickly and efficiently.

CHAPTER 26

SUMMIT STRUCTURES

Summit Structures was one of the best business ventures of my long and ambitious career. I had been in the general contracting business for eleven years, and because of personal disasters and poor business operations, I hadn't been as successful as I should have been.

By 1968, the missile sites were all finished, and I had completed two of the biggest contracts that I had ever had. There were no projects of any consequence on any of the architects' boards, and the next few years looked pretty bleak.

My brother-in-law Rex was in the same boat. We put our dreams together and decided to go for it in Denver. Rex knew an apartment developer in Boulder with whom we could contract the framing of a couple of buildings, getting us in the market for this kind of business. The superintendent couldn't make a decision on his own, so we pushed him around a little bit without his realizing it.

With a couple of good former employees and new hires, we were able to put together a good framing crew. I don't remember how we heard about our first job in Denver, but we did a couple of buildings on Happy Canyon Road. The superintendent on this job was about the best that we ever found in Denver. He knew his business and could give us a decision in minutes. We didn't have to push him around. If we had a question, we would go find Gene. If the answer was even just a little involved, he would get out his pad and draw us both the elevation and cross-section. He had a pocketful of colored pens, and he'd use a different color for every type of material. If we could see a better way of solving the problem, he would listen, and if it was indeed better than his way, he would accept and approve it immediately. If he didn't like it for some reason, he would explain why and that would be that. He was the best kind of construction superintendent. More of this kind of mutual cooperation would make the world a better place. The political partisan system completely destroys progress.

Sorry, I got carried away.

Our business grew by leaps and bounds from that moment on. We found a good banker, hired and fired hundreds of people, and had a couple of high-lift forklifts and the best equipment available. Pretty quickly, we owned our office building and a bunch of storage units. Times were good!

We had a secretary who suited our operation perfectly. Jenny was a pretty blonde about my age and could handle any situation that arose, including some of the language that flew around. One year she sent out something like seven hundred employee income tax forms. Once in a while, one of our current or former employees would come in and start complaining. The worst were generally nearly six feet tall with a forty-six-inch chest, sixteen-inch biceps, and a mop of hair to fill up the space between their size-two heads and the hard hats they had to keep on. That's not to say that all of our employees were mentally impaired; in fact, most of them went on to be very successful in other occupations. Jenny handled all of these guys with professionalism. She was so well liked that anybody who gave her any static was headed for a world of hurt.

One winter we had a couple hundred apartments under contract and more than a hundred employees at one time. That was the snowiest winter I can remember in Denver. Every Sunday, the sky would dump a bunch of snow. Every Monday morning, our foremen would use any employees who showed up to clean off the snow, and Tuesday would be too muddy or too wet to get around on the job. From Wednesday through Saturday, we could get some production. This went on for months, but Rex and I didn't waste those days that our crews couldn't work. There was new snow, and we had to go skiing. We skied almost every mountain in Colorado; Jackson Hole, Wyoming; and Park City, Utah that winter. Come spring, I figured up that if we had laid off the whole crew for the winter and paid Rex, Bobby Calhoun, and myself our weekly wages, we would have saved more than twenty thousand dollars.

In 1975 things got so slow that Bobby took his share and went to Wyoming. Rex and I sold our building and split the blanket. We had been at the right place at the right time, but it was all over. I could go on forever about the happenings in those seven years, but that would take yet another book.

CHAPTER 27

"WHY NOT?" AND "WHO, ME?"

I always liked the quotation from JFK, "The world asks, 'Why?' I question, 'Why not?'" I do know that "Why not?" has been the answer to a considerable number of my own problems and had also created some, but in all, it has prevented my demise from stagnant boredom.

I was twenty-one when I built a neat little house for my oncoming family. I was not without help, mind you. My dad gave us the lot, and Pappy was the carpenter, but I worked forty hours a week to support my family and more than forty a week on my house. I did all of the common labor; a bunch of the concrete work; and all the siding, roofing, painting, and flooring. All my energy went into creating a home for my new family. I remember that on several nights, when I finally crashed, it felt like the great big hand of God knocked me out, took the pain away, patted me on the butt, and let me sleep.

One of the first arts I learned was tying flies for trout fishing. A friend of my dad's was kind enough to get me started, and I took great pride in the fact that I could really catch fish with these little jewels. I even got good enough to go professional. I tied flies for a guy at Fort Warren (now Warren Air Force Base) for a couple of years. It paid fairly well for work done in my own house on cold winter nights. The real reward has been the countless hours of productive fun I enjoyed instead of becoming a couch potato.

My start in the building trades came pretty early. My dad's carpenter foreman, Hank Loshbaugh, hired me as a "pistol-assed kid" to do the labor work on a housing project. The two lead carpenters, Scotty Harris and Elmer Dutton, made a big impression on me. They were hard-core union of the right kind. They were good and knew they were good, and they were willing to do an honest day's work for an honest day's pay. Through the years, I held them up as the standard. Unfortunately, a whole bunch of turkeys and freeloaders are below this standard. During my tenure there, a hod carrier for the plasterer didn't show up, and the plaster crew asked Hank if they could borrow me. *Who, me?* I guess that I should have been flattered because this job was not one for a pistol-assed kid. It took a hell of a good man to shovel eighty or ninety pounds of wet mud onto a hod (a V-shaped device carried on the shoulder) and walk up a scaffold plank to the bitching bunch of plasterers. At fourteen years old, I'm not too sure that I could have lasted another day at that job.

At another point in my life, I was a professional penny stuffer. In the mid-forties, cigarettes were seventeen or eighteen cents a pack. The vending machines weren't built to give penny change, so the pennies were inserted inside the cellophane wrapping on the pack. A person put in nickels, dimes, or quarters, and the small change would come back with the cigs. I was paid a penny a pack for this menial task, but it was a whole lot better than being broke.

I also worked in a local bakery until I was assigned the job of spraying cockroaches in a bread-raising kiln. I finished the job through bullheaded determination and then walked into the office to quit. I was met by my employer saying, "You're fired!" *Who, me?*

I was completely exasperated, but it taught me a good lesson in life: always drag up *before* you get fired. Also, most of the time, any employer who fired you did you a big favor. You could go on to something that you liked or were good at instead of fighting a life of incompetence.

I have delivered local newspapers, shoveled coal into the stokers of homes and apartment heating units, mowed lawns, shoveled snow, and painted garages. I have never regretted my apprenticeship as a carpenter. I am also very pleased that a best friend and the smartest young man I ever knew (my son) learned the trade from me.

I am not a good teacher. I've been to a few seminars that impressed on me the fact that you have to say the same thing to an average person seven times before he retains it. My son and I fired a lot of average people because we were too intolerant to accept this. They always had the same look on their faces—"Who, me?"

We hired a young Mexican kid who had been through one of the Denver area trade schools. Andy was a diligent worker and was always on time to work. For the first few weeks, Rick or I would start questioning the other, asking, "Should we keep him?" *Why not?* A lot of others had bitten the dust. Andy went on to work for Rick for a good number of years and became a good friend.

We hired a framer who could have been Grizzly Adams's twin. (A few years later, another Grizz came along, but he was the ugly kind of Grizz.) We all liked the first Grizz and had a lot of respect for him. One day, a young tinner was hanging rain gutters on a house that we had completed. Things were not going well for him, and he exploded into a tirade of curse words. Grizz said, "Sounds like you when you're mad, Rick." *Who, me?* I never heard Rick explode again.

Our theory of work was similar to that of the great Vince Lombardi. "If you're not fired with enthusiasm, you will be fired, with enthusiasm." Our attitude came into play at tax time. The feds had implemented a "job tax credit." If an employer made a new hire, the first several thousand in wages were somehow credited to the employer. I think thirty-five hundred dollars was the maximum. We hired forty or fifty guys that year and only two went over the max. Some didn't even make thirty-five dollars! Rick and I have laughed ever since. Our demanding attitude had resulted in the return of enough of our prior-year taxes to pay for half of a Skylane, our dream airplane. Why not?

CHAPTER 28

OCTAVIANO AND A SKINNY KID

A skinny Mexican kept bugging me for a job on a motel addition that I had contracted. We were shingling the roof, and this guy climbed the ladder and said in broken English, "I can do that!" Any kind of roofing is not really the kind of work that any carpenter wants to suffer through. I'm not too sure that this guy had any experience, but it occurred to me that, as hungry as this guy looked, he would be happy to go to work at anything. I said, "Okay, we'll give you a shot at it."

He couldn't make out the W-4 form that I gave him, so I put my young Mexican apprentice in full charge of him.

Henry told me that the guy's name was Octaviano Mondragon but that we could call him Pancho. By the time Henry was done with him, he had become a pretty good hand at shingling. Not only that, but he didn't mind the summer sun. He finished the roof, and we were all pleased about that.

He was completely convinced that he had become a fully qualified carpenter. He started to get a little growly when we told him to do just plain old labor. One Friday night, after I gave him his paycheck, I told him to come in Saturday morning because I had a truckload of steel doors and frames that could only be delivered that morning. Sure enough, the truck was there at eight o'clock, but there was no Pancho. I had to take the entire load from the tailgate of the truck and carry it into one of the motel rooms. With every step I took, I cursed Pancho more intensely. The hot July sun almost wiped me out, and my boiling anger was no big help. In addition, I had spent the night before working with the JC Frontier Nights Committee and had naturally tipped a few beers. Cheyenne Frontier Days kicked off that evening, and I was chairman of the JC's Frontier Nights money-making project: beer sales.

I made it through that day, but my anger built along with my exhaustion. Fortunately, I was able to recuperate on Sunday. On Monday morning, one of my other employees told me that he had seen Pancho drinking beer, kicking back, and enjoying the fruits of the paycheck that I had given him on Friday night. Then I was really pissed. I immediately drove home and wrote out a check for Pancho's last few hours. I went to the job site, climbed to the roof where Pancho was working, and fired his no-good ass. Apparently, Pancho drank up his last check. When I got home that evening, I made it to the top of the short flight of stairs to our apartment when Pancho opened the apartment building's front door and started bellering, "You can't fire me! I'm a member of the carpenters union!" I knew this to be a damn lie. I said, "I already did fire you, and whatever anybody says, *you're fired*!"

He didn't take this too kindly. He rubbed the front pocket that his knife was in and said, with a threatening eye, "I'll kill you!" He turned and went out the door.

Over the next week, I walked through the Frontier Nights crowd on an almost continual basis. I kept expecting that knife to slip through my ribs as Poncho got his revenge.

Obviously, it never happened.

About a month later, I was hounded again. A young guy, maybe a high school lad, stopped almost daily to ask for a job. For a while, I had no need for any kind of laborer, but one morning we were starting a concrete pour, and the whole floor would have to be wheeled. We didn't have as many wheelbarrow operators as we needed, and about that time, there came my high school kid. I thought, *Oh, what the hell. Give the kid a chance*. I asked if he thought he could push a wheelbarrow, and he was sure that he could. I let him watch a few of our regular laborers for a bit, and he wheeled up under the ready-mix chute. The guy started putting a load into the kid's wheelbarrow. It was the usual amount, but the kid lifted the load and took about two steps before his feet went out from under him and his face splashed into the mud. I moved the wheelbarrow out of the way and helped the poor kid clean himself up. None of the other guys made fun of him because a similar thing had happened to all of us at some point or another. Nevertheless, I gave him a few bucks, and he went along his way a little bit smarter and with a little more respect for the construction laborer.

CHAPTER 29

HORSESHOE BEND MARINA

In the late seventies and early eighties, I built several buildings in Gillette. This was at the peak of the oil and coal boom, and I had three partners in my venture. Everything was leased and we were able to make the payments on our loans even though the interest was 18 percent. I thought that we had it made and moved to the Bighorn Basin with retirement in mind. I bought 160 acres and built our dream house. A realtor that I knew called me and said, "I've got a fun deal that you might be interested in in Horseshoe Bend Marina."

I purchased this deal with some friends in Denver. It was a park service leasing business, but there was also personal property such as boats and motors and a pretty nice marina service. During the first summer, Cindy and I would drive over the Bighorn Mountains on weekends to run the operation. We had big ideas and hired a couple to run the place the next summer. The female partner in the management team, who was also named Cindy, was a real winner. One time, an oil spill occurred near Horseshoe Bend, and the pipeline company that was responsible for the spill rented all four of our boats to clean up the mess. This deal alone made the summer very profitable. The oil company crew must have run one of our Honda outboard motors without keeping it in the water for cooling. The Honda outboard is pretty near bulletproof, but this crew turned this one to toast. Cindy collected around twenty five hundred dollars for the damage, and that bought a new Honda.

Another day, the newly appointed game warden came to visit. He must have been a New Jersey-type of game warden—an expression Wyoming people use to describe inexperience with our ways of doing things—because he was a mockery of the really good wardens that we had.

He had a very nice Game and Fish Department boat. As he was backing down the launching ramp, he hit his brakes too hard and dumped his boat onto the concrete. Cindy's husband helped him get his boat in the water. Then, as he was climbing off the dock, he dropped his revolver into the lake, and we had to get one of the local kids to dive for it.

The business was a fun deal for a while, but one of the partners from Denver decided that he wanted to run the place the next summer. This guy was a great drinking buddy, but he wasn't worth sour owl shit when it came to managing anything. As far as I was concerned, the whole deal became sour. I really think that we could have made a big success of our Horseshoe Bend endeavor if the whole economy hadn't gone so bad and our brilliant government hadn't bailed out all the savings and loans and knocked down the energy business.

Over a few brokenhearted times, years of sometimes back-breaking work, and the dedication of my partner Johnny Kahler, we finally bailed out our rental buildings in Gillette and have been able to enjoy some of the returns.

CHAPTER 30

THE 48ERS AND THE WRINKLE CLUB

Two organizations are of great pleasure to me and my old pals. The 48ers are a group of guys who graduated from Cheyenne High School in 1948 and get together for a monthly luncheon. It is very interesting that at least half of us had to leave Cheyenne to pursue our various livelihoods. Wyoming has always been a boom-or-bust state, but Cheyenne is probably the most stable city of all. Nevertheless, almost all of us were lured away by better career opportunities, the armed services, or existence demands. The really interesting part is that so many of us wanted to retire in Cheyenne.

We have anywhere from ten to twenty-five people at each meeting of the 48ers. We also just had our sixtieth class reunion and had a great turnout. My wife, Cindy, went to her fiftieth and said all of her classmates were fat and using oxygen and went home early. But my classmates were joined together, singing, and having a great time.

The class of '48 was the first class to go through high school without World War II going on since it began. Every guy had to register for the draft, and a few went straight into one service or another. I joined the Naval Reserve and served for five years. Most of the rest took the same kind of path. When we get to reminiscing, it's so interesting what is brought up—things that were of no consequence at the time but have been embedded in our minds for so many years. We do not discriminate, one way or the other, with regard to what year a person actually graduated. We all grew up with WWII in the back of our minds and well remember the sacrifices that our older brothers and sisters made. We all remember the shortages of things that were needed for the war effort. There were rationing stamps for all these things, including sugar, meat, gasoline, tires, and so many things that we take for granted today. Levi's were as scarce as hen teeth. As I remember, there were only two stores in town that offered them. As soon as the word got out that one of these stores had some in stock, the popular sizes would be gone in a flash. They always had the big sizes because there were not many fat kids; I don't remember anyone who was obese. McDonald's hadn't been created yet, and there sure were no other fast-food joints. And there was no prejudice because there was no one to be prejudiced about.

Now, the Wrinkle Club is a little different story. We are a bunch of old farts who gather for coffee every weekday morning. We piss and moan, curse aches and pains, put up with old women talking about old men, stir up whatever trouble we can, share breakfast sandwiches, laugh at or with one another, and thoroughly enjoy the comradery. This group includes several of the 48ers and other people who are between fifty-five and ninety years old. We've lost some of our troops but actively promote new membership. Most are Wyoming natives. Oddly enough, we have almost as many natives from Rawlins as any other town in Wyoming. One was a sheep rancher-turned-politician—probably the only politician who is as close to honest as anybody I know. We also have an ex-banker, a former school superintendent, and locally we have a retired Air Force colonel, a retired real estate broker, a retired electrician, and of course, me. There are occasional drop-ins who add to our story. We welcome any new old farts to become members. It's hard to find people who have reached our status in life. Our average age is about eighty, so obits are quite frequent.

CHAPTER 31

CARSON

Carson could say more filthy words in one sentence than most foul-mouthed goons could say after giving the effort some thought. I met him when I was the superintendent for a tenant-finish contractor at McCarran International Airport in Las Vegas. The work at the airport had slowed up a bit, but my employer wanted to keep me employed because he knew that I could bail his dumb ass out of any airline remodeling project. He had purchased a high-dollar lot in a double-high-dollar subdivision on which he intended to build a mansion. The trouble was that he and his financier wife were headed for divorce. I had figured the cost of the house for him, but he wouldn't believe me. Be that as it may, he contracted a framing crew to complete the stick frame of his new mansion.

Enter Carson.

I knew him, and he knew me. We had never met, but we immediately understood each other. That happens quite often in the building industry and, I would hope, in any other intelligent industry.

My laborer Ryland and I got the foundation and slab done with the help of a Mexican plumber and a very black and very big tinner who worked for an Italian contractor that had no respect for any tradesman. The contractor had, apparently, been raised by mafia goons. The only reasons he had been successful were mob graft and one smart daughter, Gina. She was the brains of the whole operation. She giggled a bit when I called her father a big, stupid, incompetent, no-account, miserable son of a bitch. And he was! He looked at me like I was a dead man. I returned his glare with my own look that said, *Just try it!* (Another overconfident shot in life.) With his connections in Las Vegas, he could have wasted me within hours, but he didn't want to spend a marker for a challenge from an old German. This miserable little punk took several shots at me. I loved his daughter, though. Gina was everything that her daddy wasn't.

Anyway, Carson was tough looking. He had an eternal grin and was ready for a big laugh or a big fight at a moment's notice. He and his brother were really good at the carpenter trade. It's always interesting to observe the differences in the training and methods used in each particular part of the building trade.

I had never swung a hammer that weighed less than sixteen ounces, and these were considered finish hammers. But Carson and his whole crew had thirteen-ounce hammers. I asked him how the hell he could drive a sixteen-penny nail with a tack hammer, and he scoffed. However, he made my point for me several weeks later. Carson, his brother, and a big jock hired hand were struggling to place their prefabbed stair horse on the promenade of this ill-conceived house, and Carson bellered to me that they needed some help. I let them grunt and groan for some time and then sauntered up the ladder to help. As they had the stair horse in the exact position and three sixteen-penny nails set and ready to drive, Carson bellered, "Stab it!"

I was standing at the top of the landing and waited until the guys were about to collapse. I swung my twenty-four-ounce knurled-face framing hammer two times, drove two big nails, and walked. The big jock's eyes were lying on his cheeks. He looked at Carson and said, "He missed!!" What? Carson shrugged his shoulders and said, "You saw it!"

My reaction was the result of years of experience—and a certain amount of dumb luck. I hadn't driven a sixteen-penny nail in years but sure impressed a young, strong, tradesman-to-be. At that moment, I felt like my own young-life mentor, Tony Linden. It was fun to think that this young buck might remember me the way I remember Tony.

Carson and I had a few differences of opinion but still respected each other. I didn't want to swing my framing hammer at him, and I don't think he wanted to kill me either.

He had a wife who was entirely devoted to this ornery bastard. She had two kids from an earlier marriage, and I think that marriage had not been too happy. Carson was rough, tough, and ready compared to what Tony had told me about the refined ways of his wife's first husband. Regardless, Carson and Toni were nearly a perfect match.

Carson and Tony were from Maryland and seemed entirely displaced in Las Vegas. I asked Carson what brought him to Vegas, and he told me that a Maryland judge had told him to cross seven state lines and not look back. Enough said! You really didn't want to go anywhere with Carson and Toni if you weren't ready for trouble.

They loved the Paddlewheel in Las Vegas. On Friday nights, the casino served crab legs on an all-you-can eat basis, and Carson and Toni knew how to eat crab legs. The number of crab legs that they could devour was almost unbelievable. I had never seen anybody who could grab a crab leg, snap it in three places, and clean it to the shell like these two. As soon as our order was served, they would ask for more. They were pretty demanding when it came to service, and it was interesting to watch the waiters. After the first reorder, the waiters would scamper to bring the next, completely intimidated by these two. I don't remember an evening there that they didn't reorder at least six times. The Paddlewheel management shuddered every time Carson and Tony walked through the door.

The contractor that I was serving as a superintendent for was a perfect example of the "screw the subcontractors, material men, employees, owners and anyone else in order to make greater profits" approach to business. He was greed personified.

Carson had been lured by the promise of an airport contract. He had the contract for the demolition of one of the satellite buildings at ramp level at McCarran.

My boss hired another superintendent without doing me the courtesy of telling me. Carson asked me who this turkey was. I had no idea then but soon found out that the new superintendent was totally full of bullshit (he was a PhD at BS but still a likeable sort).

At that time, we had contracts with Southwest Airlines, American Airlines, Delta Airlines, Pizza Hut, and a major candy provider. My employer expected me to supervise the operation and do all the carpentry labor for the American Airlines remodel. It was a challenge!

But at that time in my life, I needed all the challenges that were available. I never had any problem with doing lots of hard work, either physical or mental, because of the things that were happening to me back home.

Carson's original contract was the demolition of a ramp level interior in one of the satellite buildings. He was to take care of all the salvageable material. Upon close examination, Carson saw a lot of brass railings, posts, barriers and more. He was no dummy. He and his crew tore out all the brass in the first couple of days and stacked it in a vacant room. He rented a trailer and pulled it in with his old GMC pickup, loaded all the brass in double time, and asked me to call a security escort to go with him to the gate. Ordinarily, security would have scrutinized this load for several days, but I had earned a certain amount of credibility and they escorted Carson's loot out the south gate. He got a real nice bundle of money for his efforts. My boss would have had a conniption if he had known, but he never did.

My boss was infamous for retaining subcontractor payments for any reason. Carson and his brother Willy had stopped by the office to pick up their check, but there was no check to be had. Our secretary Linda was very apologetic, but that didn't satisfy Carson and Willy very much.

We had a high-dollar radio system at the time, and as Willy walked out of the office, he lifted the office radio. I stopped by for my check and found Linda in total desperation. Her scaredy-cat voice squealed, "Carson stole my radio! The boss will fire me!" If my check hadn't been there, I might have stolen her fax machine.

"Bob, what am I going to do?" she asked.

It was Friday night, so I knew there were only two places that Carson and Willy would be.

I said, "Linda, be cool. I'll get your radio back before five." She wanted to hug and kiss me, but I escaped before she could.

I drove to the Four Leaf Clover and lucked out. Lo and behold, there were Carson and Willy. I hadn't been through the door long enough to get my eyes accustomed to the light when Carson came to stand in front of me with a radio in his hand. I said, "Carson, you guys are a pain in the butt. I'll be back in about forty minutes, and you'd better have me a couple scotch and waters." He saluted and said, "Aye, aye, Captain."

By the time I got back, the two of them were a little more drunk. I quaffed my two drinks, and then I had two more. I was enjoying the minute!

Carson waved his arm, and a very pretty woman came over and sat down at our table. Then Carson motioned to me. There was no doubt in my mind that she was no hooker, but what was going on? She said, "Look at the clover," pointing to the wall. I did, and she started a pencil drawing on a big artist pad. I knew that she was doing a portrait of my homely face. I didn't know why, but she kept telling me to look at the clover. After only about a scotch and a half, she quit looking. She scribbled for a few more minutes and then handed Carson the portrait. He paid her and grinned. Nothing that Carson ever did would surprise me. After a few more snorts, he handed me the drawing, and I could hardly believe it. I had never been photogenic, and I had never thought of myself as handsome. This gal had transformed my average-at-best face with an oversized nose into a pretty classy-looking portrait.

Carson and Tony were a great diversion in spare time. They had lived a lot classier life before, but they were plumb happy with the carefree life that they had started living since.

I had pulled my big honker Parteaux boat to Vegas, and Carson was intrigued by it. Ryland and sons had helped me put a 440 Dodge engine in, but we had never finished the job. Carson couldn't wait to go to Lake Mead and light this beauty. We worked one weekend to make sure it would start and run. I had a big problem with a jet way (moveable bridge from terminal to plane) at McCarran and couldn't get away to run a jet boat. Carson asked if I cared if he took the Parteaux to the lake. I knew that, one way or another, he'd get the job done. "No problem, Carson," I said. "Go ahead!"

On Monday morning, I heard him say, "That boat sounds like a screamer, but it won't pull a sick whore off a piss pot!" Something was definitely wrong. We took off the next day at noon, pulled the boat to the lake, and, sure enough, it sounded somewhat rough but good. I had known that boat from the first keel through several engines. We pulled the engine hood, and I had Carson light it. After about three revolutions, I knew what the problem was. The right bank of plugs was grounding out on the exhaust manifold. It was firing on only four cylinders. "Let's go home," I said.

We parked the Parteaux under a big shade tree and swapped the manifolds—right to left and left to right. It was still plenty warm and light out, so we headed back to the lake. We gave the engine one crank, and it spit fire for a second or two before it became the screamer that it was supposed to be. I'm not sure that Carson didn't spit a little fire himself when he heard that thunder. We did have a little fun in Vegas!

One morning after I had retired and was wondering what to do next, I drove out to Lake Mead. I had made a questionable decision to sell my old "power wagon" and bought a two-wheel-drive pickup of the same vintage but with far less wear and tear.

I had driven some of the shoreline and was pretty much on the weathered beach. My desire for exploring had, once more, put me in a precarious position. The little dry wash that I had crossed to this dead end had trapped me with its loose gravel and steep slope. The farther up that hill that I tried to go, the farther I slid to a washed-out ravine that could have tipped me and my pickup into deep trouble. I couldn't move either way without getting into more trouble. The marina was in easy sight. The particular place I had ended up was only across the mouth of this big water bay from the marina. I decided that it would be easier to swim a couple hundred yards than to walk the six or seven miles on the ground. I pulled my Levi's behind me on a nylon string because I was swimming in my birthday suit. As I approached, I chose the closest beach, pulled on my Levi's, and walked to the marina store. Its proprietor was not the most helpful soul that I had ever met, and I decided to call Cinder to ask her to take my scrawny, naked ass out of this unfriendly environment.

Our apartment was about thirty miles from the Lake Mead Marina. Cinder was not very excited about driving a rescue mission but decided I might be worth the effort. She picked me up in due time, and we returned to our humble abode.

I knew that any vehicular help that I might get would end up in the same pickle as my truck. It would take at least forty feet of tow rope, probably fifty, to get my truck out of there. I called several suppliers, and my final choice was a knowledgeable rope supplier. I bought sixty feet of nylon rope along with the connecting hardware for towing and then called Carson.

Any help that I would get from Carson would come after noon. This was summertime, and every tradesman will finish his days' work before noon if any part of it is in the sun. About two-thirty, Carson called and said, "You want me to bail you out again?" I told him, "Yeah, but I always have enough beer to do it!"

I don't think that the beer or circumstances would make any difference. Our friendship would win out. He picked me up in his GM pickup. Tony was with him. We drove to the tricky cove, and Carson said, "I ain't going down there!" I knew he would say that. I told him, "Back down the trail till you're scared that this Jimmy pig can't make it out!"

If there was no challenge, there probably would be no help. Carson gave me that "f—you" look and backed up closer than I would have expected. I got my big plastic bag out and unreeled sixty feet of brand new, one-inch nylon rope with a chain and hook on both ends. Carson finally gave me a look of approval. We didn't have to make plans. The die was cast.

I handed one end to Carson and scurried to hook the other end to my old Dodge. I hadn't even started my engine when Carson started uphill. The nylon rope stretched, and I was on my way to somewhere. But "somewhere" ended up to be in the washed-out area that I didn't want to be in. Carson had run to the switchback and, of course, had to stop. This could not have been worse for me and my big old Dodge. We were dangling over the washout.

I crawled out of the passenger side and hoped that that the weight transfer wouldn't dump "Big Iron" into the hole. Carson changed his direction and was ready again. I said, "Hey, Cars, wait until I get the engine started before you start pulling."

I might as well have said, "Hit it" because Carson waited only until I was in the driver's seat. Somehow I drove backward to the switchback, turned sideways, hit the brakes, and stalled Carson's truck. He hollered, "Evidently, you're happy!"

Sometimes he really pissed me off. It's a good thing that we had great, mutual respect for each other because if I would have hit him, I would have broken my fist. If he would have hit me, he'd have broken my face. I knew that I could drive out from where I was and damn sure didn't want any more help. I was plumb lucky to have survived this much.

Carson was certainly an experience in life. He was an honest, hardworking, challenging individual who made a few mistakes, not unlike myself.

CHAPTER 32

OFFICERS CLUB

In the early sixties, a lot of remodeling jobs were being offered for bid at Fort Francis E. Warren. A bid invitation was published for the remodel of the officers club. This was of particular interest to me because of all the great social fun that I had experienced in my "growing up" years. The school district had arranged with the base officials to allow school kids to have a dance at this fancy facility on one Friday per month. Junior high school kids (grades seven through nine) had the place from seven o'clock to nine o'clock, and the high school kids had it from nine o'clock through eleven o'clock. These dances were known as the Hops, and they required formal attire—coat and tie for guys and a formal dress for the gals, just like on *Happy Days*. A few years later, we were privileged to go to the same facility because my sister married an officer in the National Guard. All these memories were of great days for those of us who had been in the right place at the right time.

The remodeling job was even more interesting to me because the architect was one of my favorites. This job was not under the authority of the Corps of Engineers but was to be supervised by the base authorities.

My bid was not the lowest, but the base procurement office was not on friendly terms with my competitor, the low bidder. An alternative bid came in for the new bar equipment, which gave the contracting officer the flexibility to rebid with the three low-bidding contactors. I knew that my closest competitor was infamous for bidding a job at a ridiculously low amount and then tacking on huge "change orders" that could have easily been anticipated. I also knew that the architect and the base construction officials would rather not deal with my competitor and that I had a certain edge. My bar equipment supplier was greatly helpful when it came to pricing and knowledge and his new pricing madehe deciding vote in my favor. Getting the contract came down to a matter of few dollars, and I let the competitor know that he was not the only fish in the pond.

This job required a bunch of demolition before improvements could be made. For some reason or another, I have always liked to tear things apart. I was the first guy on the crew to swing the first sledgehammer and get the crew into a "demo" frame of mind. We signed the contract with the contracting officer. This particular job was to be done for a quasi-governmental entity but supervised by the procurement office and the officer's club management. It was my plan to get the demolition work done first so that the real remodel work could be initiated.

The old special designed ceiling over the dance floor was to be removed so that a new acoustical one could be installed. The specifications were not very clear, so I opted to drop the whole ceiling in one big shebang even though there was no doubt in my mind that the architect and contracting officer would frown on this idea. We brought my plywood concrete forms in to cover the polyfilm and protect the hardwood dance floor. The next step was seeing how many of the hanger wires we could dispose of before the big bang. My guys had it all figured, and their plan sounded feasible. They had all of the permanent hanger wires removed and the whole ceiling ready to fall. The theory was that we could have one carpenter on each of the six remaining wires around the perimeter and cut them all at the same time.

I really didn't want anybody to know that I was aware of the plan, let alone that I had approved it. As I was walking down the sidewalk to my truck, lo and behold, a big crash noise came from the interior. I quickened my step. I knew nothing.

The contracting officer never knew anything about this incident, but then he never knew anything.

The top sergeant caught me as I walked in the door the next morning trying to look as innocent as possible. He said, "Buenger, you dingbat! It will take my crew a week to dust and clean all the glasses!" I said, "What do you mean, Sarge?" He grinned and told me that this was going to cost me. It did, but not near as much as the time and labor that would have been spent taking the ceiling down another way. I had learned that if I could please the top sergeant, I didn't have to worry about the contracting officer.

There were some shenanigans going on between the contracting officer and an old chick from town who had been a child actress. She was a decent-looking old skillet and had the poor major huffing, puffing, and pissing on the lamppost. Most of the interior finish was not part of my contract, so I had no say when this old broad sold the major a cheap carpet at a ridiculous price. This little deal cost the major his position and probably his commission.

It never ceases to amaze me that top leaders can let their peckers lead them into ruin. There are a lot of nice ladies out there. 'Nuff said.

My brother-in-law Rex was on leave from the Army for a good number of days, and I put him on my payroll because he was always good at whatever he did. He and I were measuring the length of a structural beam that was to carry part of the balcony. I had my hundred-foot tape in my hand but didn't want to crawl down a ladder to carry an end to him. I hollered, "I'll hold the end and throw the case to you." No problem! I unrolled a bunch of tape and threw the case to Rex. It was more than thirty feet, so I had to throw the case pretty hard. Rex saw my throw but lost sight of the case, and it hit him in the face just above an eyebrow. He bled like a stuck hog. Sarge took him to a base doctor, who stitched him up.

About a week later, Rex and I were working on a screening wall in the entryway that consisted of vertical and horizontal two-inch walnut. I was working on a sawhorse on the entry side, and Rex was putting a member near the floor on the other side. I accidentally dropped a chunk of walnut, and it hit Rex's thumb dead center. His thumb blew up like a little purple balloon. He started dancing around like the Native American that he claimed to be. He had done about the same thing to me previously, but I did a far better job. I knew from prior experience that the only way to relieve the throbbing was to get the blood out from under the thumbnail, so I took an electric drill and devised a little piece of wood to prevent me from drilling through anything more than just the thumbnail. I could never get anything done if I was nice to him, so I said, "Come over here, you big dumby He could see what I had planned and stuck out his thumb. The drill bit was sharp and small, and I only had to touch the nail with it. The blood squirted out, and Rex said the pain subsided significantly. I told him, "Now keep your damn thumb out of the way!" I thought that he might take a swing at me, but he didn't.

My sergeant friend was Mexican and was furnishing a coffee break for us one morning. My apprentice Henry was also Mexican. He and Sarge were joking around with each other when one of my younger carpenters said, "Henry, Sarge calls you a Mexican, and you both laugh like hell. I call you a Mexican, and you call me a son of a bitch."

The job came out very well. The Sarge and base engineers were happy. I can't remember any building contract that I enjoyed like that one. I ran into Sarge at a restaurant after he had retired, and we renewed our old friendship.

CHAPTER 33

REX

No book regarding my time on earth would be complete without relating my experiences with the person who was my friend, brother-in-law, business partner, and quite a few other descriptions that might not be appropriate for any book. I had known Rex, along with his two sisters, throughout our growing-up years. I married Glenna, and we parented a daughter and a son. I didn't really know Rex until I started dating Glenna. Rex and I were both raised in a hunting, fishing, and generally outdoor lifestyle. We hunted for pheasants, ducks, deer, antelope, and whatever else might suit our fancy. The only trouble with hunting with Rex was that he couldn't stand to see a bird on a telephone or power pole. He had to shoot at it even if it scared away legal game that we had been stalking for six hours. No amount of screaming or cussing would faze him. I always thought that I was a better marksman than he, but when he was in the service, he was chosen to be one of the top marksmen in the armed forces. My boasting hardly compared with his cabinet full of trophies. Sometimes he really pissed me off.

Somehow, we were always fighting. Never in a real serious mode, I made this wise decision when Rex's sixteenth birthday rolled around. He was four years younger than I, but he passed me in stature about that time. I stopped by to take Glenna out, and Rex had thugged a couple pairs of boxing gloves that he was anxious to try out. I'd learned a few moves from my good friend Mid, but I learned a few more from Rex. He was sixteen and I was twenty, but it didn't take long for me to find out that he had indeed grown up. Between his new reach and my big nose, I realized that boxing was damn sure not the way to tangle assholes with this guy.

Anytime he was on leave from the service, I'd hire him no matter what project was going on. He could always adapt to the job at hand, even if there were a few wrecks along the way.

When he got out of the service, he started to contract on his own in Laramie, but that area dried up at the same time as Cheyenne did. We joined forces and founded Summit Structures, which I described earlier.

We skied together a whole bunch while we were in Colorado, and in the summer we took our boats to Wyoming. There was always less traffic there.

One year we were not creating enough travel expenses, so we took a trip to Mexico City. I met a really foxy schoolteacher who was attracted to me and my lifestyle. I wasn't divorced yet, though, and that would have created more trouble than I needed at the time. Our endeavor in Colorado was a great success but dried up, as building booms are famous for doing. We shared a bunch of boom-time success, as well as the recreation bonuses that were involved.

Our shop and office was adjacent to a waterway that was dry most of the year, providing a natural playground for dirt bikes. We got a hell of a deal on three Suzuki 250s—one each for Rex, Calhoun, and me. Bobby and Rex both had experience, and I was determined to become a dirt biker no matter how many wrecks it took. We had one framing crew that was obsessed with bikes. When they all came to our office, it was much like the Hells Angels, so we had to put a big whoa on the visits. We took quite a few trips to the South Platte River trails. I never did figure out how we all lived through these adventures, especially me.

Rex and I went to Aspen for more adventure. We skied Aspen Mountain, Snowmass, and the Aspen Highlands. The Highlands had a lift that went to the top of Loge Peak, and a sign at this lift said, "Don't take this lift unless you are an expert." We got to the top and started down. The start of this ski run made a lot of people rethink their expert status. The only way to get to the rest of the mountain was to go over a ridge about six feet wide and a hundred yards long. One side of the ridge meant six months in the hospital, and the other side meant sudden death. A solid line of skiers sidestepped this skinny trail. We fell in line, but I could see Rex getting awful fidgety. All of a sudden, he bailed off the trail and traversed the slope. If I hadn't had a few snorts of Catawba earlier, I never would have followed. We got by this line of sidesteppers, risking our future life in trade for an hour of sidestepping—not a wise decision, but we lucked out.

Rex had great little sixteen-foot boat with a 289 Ford engine and V drive. It was probably the most dependable ski boat I ever encountered. He probably would have kept it forever if a poor little rich boy hadn't come along selling a screamer race boat. Rex had to have it and sold his dependable little ski boat. I sure screwed up by not buying it, but I opted to build a twenty-one-foot jet boat. It was a great boat but cost me a fortune to build and another fortune to drive.

Rex worked on his new racer for a week before we went to the lake. It didn't live up to what Rex expected, so we found our super mechanic. Mel tweaked it for a while and announced that it was ready for a test drive. The surface of the water was perfect, so Rex took the wheel. Mel and his wife climbed aboard, and I had to go along. Rex headed up a straightaway with no other traffic with the engine wound out at full throttle. He let off the cavitations plates, and the boat felt like it had just fired its afterburners

Mel's wife had an empty beer can between her legs, and the second we took off she crushed that beer can. When we got back to the beach, Mel picked up the can and said, "Damn, Judy, why don't you do a number like that on me once in a while?"

Rex also worked to be a competitor as a bull rider and traveled with a bunch of other aspiring riders. I helped him down on the nastiest bull that I can remember at the National Western Rodeo in Denver. This bull had been ridden the full eight seconds only a very few times.

When Rex left company from this double-ugly critter, he landed in a very vulnerable position, planted with his head and shoulder on the turf and his legs in the air. A rodeo clown named Buddy Heaton stepped between the savage critter and Rex. He smacked the bull in the face with his hat as he went by, diverting the bull's charge and saving Rex a bunch of discomfort and maybe his life.

Due to the lifestyle that we both lived, there is no question why our bodies, joints, bones, and other facilities are just plain worn out. It's not because either of us were couch potatoes. Active and physical lives contributed to our longevity. We sure lived and had a lot of fun destroying the physical features that we were blessed with.

With the aid of relatives and friends, we were able to attend the memorial for Rex's older sister Ginny. It was a trip down memory lane for both of us. Lots of old playmates were there. Rex brought up the fact that we used to walk the two-by-four wall plates three or four stories up in the air. Now we have some problem just walking. A friend is someone who knows all your faults and likes you in spite of them. Rex and I qualify in either position. He is my friend. Our relationship survived many interesting and adventurous years.

CHAPTER 34

JAKE AND JARROD

When we first moved into the house that I built when we went back to Cheyenne, we didn't know any of our new neighbors. I was building a fence for a dog that we hadn't found yet because this was part of the dream we had had since we had to move away. I was in our backyard when two little guys came over to see what was happening. They had a wagon in which they were taking turns pulling each other. I said, "Hi, guys. Where are you from?" They were not a bit bashful and pointed to the house next door. The smaller of the two said, "I'm Jake, and he's Jarrod." There was no question that I liked these two. I said, "You guys are welcome to come over here anytime." This was the beginning of a long friendship. The longer we knew each other, the stronger our bond became. I helped solve a couple of problems for them, and they came to believe that I would help them anytime. I was delighted!

One day, I said, "What are you two honyocks up to?" They related to that term immediately. They were from Nebraska, where it was used by their uncles and grandparents for young boys who were special to them. Their parents were both from farm families in Nebraska and pretty well knew how the world went around.

Their dad, Doug, worked with a cellular company and was out of town quite often. Mary, their mother, was really a pretty gal. Sometimes she was more of an older sister than a mom and would go out in the yard to play with the boys, but they always knew who was boss. She told us that she had grown up with five older brothers and knew how to fight like any boy. There was little doubt of that.

The boys had a sandbox in their backyard. Cindy and I watched these two guys move this sand pile into and out of the wagon more times than we could count. Not only this, but when a good size snowstorm with a northerly wind came through, it would create deep snowbanks on the south side of the road that ran by our houses. They would dig tunnels into the snow and create little igloo-type dens. Their digging antics were sure fun to watch.

Both boys would come over whenever things were too quiet at home, and they would do anything to help me. Whenever I sat down in my La-Z-Boy, one of them was bound to say, "What are we going to do now?" It was always a challenge because I liked to have them around anytime.

One day I looked out, and Mary and the boys were busy conducting a gopher eradication program. That particular year, these pests were on a destruction mission. The boys searched for their holes, and Mary had a sack full of rodent bombs, which could be placed in a rodent hole and had a fuse to be lit. The theory was that the gases produced by these bombs would kill any critters inside the holes. This method worked great but was too expensive to stop the infestation of these pests, so the boys came over to discuss the problem. Their idea was to direct the exhaust from their dad's diesel truck into the holes, but that was a little extreme. I, however, had a little Briggs and Stratton engine that smoked pretty badly. So we devised a gopher death machine. Jake and Jarrod were really enthused and got totally involved. They picked out the biggest gopher mound, and we set our device with the little engine's exhaust directed down the gopher hole. After an hour or two, our area looked like a volcano was about to explode. Exhaust smoke was belching from holes that we didn't know were there. We didn[t see any gophers around there for a long time.

Jake came over one evening and wanted to build a science project. He had visions of a solar-powered generator. I didn't completely understand what solar power was, but he and I built a contraption of his design. I don't know what the end result was, but his teacher had to at least give him a giant E for effort.

Both boys came to visit early one morning. I really hadn't had time to do my morning chores, and my hair was standing all over the place. Jarrod, who rarely made any comment on anything, blurted out, "Well, good morning, *Hairdo*!"

The two of them spread the word that I could fix anything that was busted. They brought all kinds of projects from the rest of the neighborhood, and I always did my best to help validate their claims. I was generally able to do what they asked, but one day they brought a neighborhood friend who had a piece-of-junk soapbox racer. It was falling apart in quite a number of places. The metal that it was made of was some kind of cheap alloy. I told them that I would do whatever I could to salvage the thing but that my welding was not up to par with good steel, let alone with alloy. They came over a couple of days later, and I asked them what had happened with their friend's racer. They laughed and said, "It fell apart before he got it home." This failure didn't diminish their trust in me, though, because they knew from the start that it was pretty much a losing battle, and they laughed as hard as I did.

I hired them to help me install the siding on the garage addition that I was building. I had an air nailer and trusted them to use it. They had some competition over who got to use it and got into a couple of squabbles that I knew were not good. I said, "Okay, boys, we're going to knock off this afternoon and start all over again in the morning. We don't need any problems with the use of the air gun. I'll give you both a dollar an hour raise if you share the gun equally and quit squabbling. We don't need any fingers nailed to the wall!" That solved the problem immediately, and the boys were savvy enough to remember the lesson.

Time flies too fast, and those two boys were becoming young men. I got a little reprieve when Mary had one more boy named Jackson. He was a carbon copy of Jake and Jarrod.

Jarrod was never much interested in fishing; on the other hand, Jake was really interested. They were over at our house one evening when I had my whole fly-tying outfit out, with all the material and equipment in full view, and was adding to my overabundant collection. Of course, they said, "Whatcha doing?" This was about the last thing that we hadn't already explored. Jake had a profound interest and Jarrod didn't care about the "what for," but of course I had to show them how to tie flies and let them try whatever creatures they could think of. They invented quite a few that were not too useful except for the fact that they had learned something new.

I asked Jake if he wanted to go fishing in my boat. Of course, he did and wanted to bring a friend. No problem. But the day's fishing was not too good. A couple of days later, he and his friend stopped by and asked me to go with them. That was a new one; I accepted immediately. We headed west of town, and they showed me more cricks in which to catch brookies than I knew existed.

I had visions of mentoring another of their family members, but, sadly for me, the whole family moved to Texas. Their new house was of their design and near a big lake where they could boat. Doug found a job there that he was pleased with. They all have been back to visit, and I love to see them all. They made for a delightful chapter in an old man's life.

I must have had a lot of fun in my eighty-one years, because they say that time flies when you are having fun. There are still a bunch of Wyoming tales in my old Kraut head. If only I could sit by a big cottonwood campfire. Cottonwood smoke is almost like the "funny weed" to an old kid from Wyoming.

AUTHOR BIOGRAPHY

Flukes and fate are still following Robert Buenger, the grandson of a Wyoming homesteader. His ventures have slowed down somewhat these days, but only the final curtain will put an end to this storyteller.

His dad, Bing, was a true Wyoming citizen, wildlife enthusiast, and protector of everything that is precious to Wyoming people. Robert was raised in this type of environment. Bing started his son in the tradition of providing wild game for his family. Robert had two freezer lockers and boxes when he was first married, and his kids probably never tasted beef until their early teen years. Football and other high school sports were not part of Robert's interests since they did not tend toward an outdoor life. In lue of sports, Robert filled his weekends with hunting everything from rabbits to elk. Trout fishing, horses and dogs filled the rest of his free time. Robert was a boy scout during high school. During this time, he earned the Eagle Scout Award and was elected governor for a day. In all, it was a pretty good way for a Wyoming kid to grow up.

In Robert's day, the armed services were a part of almost any young man's life. Robert served in the naval reserve for five years but was never called to active duty. An apprenticeship at the local carpenter's union ultimately started Robert's lifelong business as a general building contractor. Robert now lives in Cheyenne, Wyoming with his wife Cindy.